Get Their Attention!

29.

Related titles of interest:

Behaviour Management in the Classroom
Sandra Newell and David Jeffery

Improving Behaviour and Raising Self Esteem in the Classroom
Giles Barrow, Emma Bradshaw and Trudi Newton

Managing Behaviour in Classrooms
John Visser

The Art of Teaching Peacefully
Michelle MacGrath

Get Their Attention!

How to Gain Pupils' Respect
and Thrive as a Teacher

Sean O'Flynn and Harry Kennedy
Revised for the English edition by
Michelle MacGrath

David Fulton Publishers

David Fulton Publishers Ltd
The Chiswick Centre, 414 Chiswick High Road, London W4 5TF

www.fultonpublishers.co.uk

First published in Great Britain in 2003 by
David Fulton Publishers

10 9 8 7 6 5 4 3 2 1

Note: The right of the authors to be identified as the authors of this work
has been asserted by them in accordance with the Copyright, Designs
and Patents Act 1988.

David Fulton Publishers is a division of Granada Learning Limited,
part of Granada plc.

British Library Cataloguing in Publication Data
A catalogue record for this book is available from the British Library.

ISBN 1 84312 080-1

Typeset by Pantek Arts Ltd, Maidstone, Kent
Printed and bound in Great Britain

Contents

Book Structure   viii
Acknowledgement   viii
Preface to the English edition   ix

Preface to Parts 1 and 2   **1**

Part 1 On becoming a teacher   **5**

Application and interview   5
New to the school   9
Initial class contact   9
The start-up routine   12
Desperate measures!   17
Timing the lesson   18
Asking and taking questions   20
Making announcements and giving instructions   22
Pacing   27
Tests   28
Tools of the trade   29
'With-it-ness'   31
Homework   32
Files   34
Cover lessons   34
Staff meetings   35
The staffroom   37
Parents' evenings   38
School reports   39
Extracurricular activities   41
Educational visits   41

Part 2 Communicating authority in the classroom   45

Combating behaviour problems   48
Confidence   53
Dealing with trouble   53
Detention   57
School Code of Discipline   57
Exclusion   58
Triangulation   59
Meeting the parents   60
Recording   61
Emotional clarity   61
Coercive classroom management style   62

Preface to Part 3   65

Part 3 Enabling approaches to classroom management   69

The role of self-esteem in classroom management   70
Things teachers can do to raise the self-esteem of students 74
Teaching a 'difficult' class   80
Some suggestions when teaching a 'difficult' class   84
Maintaining relationship with students   91
Constructive confrontation   93
You're not listening to me!   104
Motivation   108
Some characteristic traits of children from troubled homes 112
Strategies 'low achievers' use for coping with school   117
Some suggestions on taking mixed ability classes   124
Specific learning difficulties: dyslexia and dyspraxia   129

Part 4 **Teaching as a career** **133**

Phases in the teaching career 133
Minding ourselves 138
Strategies for thriving in the job 140

References **146**

Appendices **147**

Book Structure

Parts 1 and 2 are written primarily for teachers who are beginning their teaching careers. These sections suggest coercive approaches to classroom management which may be helpful and appropriate to teachers at the beginning of their career, the start of the school year or when establishing themselves in a school.

If you are an experienced teacher, you may wish to go straight to Part 3. This advocates more advanced, enabling approaches to classroom management which can be used once a teacher has gained a satisfactory level of classroom experience.

The final sections deal with issues such as career planning, strategies for thriving in the job, and stress management.

In this text, gender-specific pronouns and adjectives are used interchangeably, and are understood in all cases to mean persons of both genders.

Acknowledgement

We are grateful to those people, who from the start, recognised the value of what we are attempting to do in this book, and who have been generous in their support and encouragement.

Preface to the English edition

In preparing this book for the English edition I was very aware that it is one of the books I wish I could have read early on in teaching. It would have saved me much stress, heartache and misplaced energy and would have helped me improve my teaching immensely, without having to learn so many things the hard way. Although it was written in Ireland, the issues it deals with are universally relevant to all teachers: how to relate effectively to young people and manage classes in ways that promote learning. Without these two elements, teaching is ineffective. It is, I think, an essential and pleasurable read.

Michelle MacGrath
July 2003

Preface to Parts 1 and 2

'tis all in the eye

▓ Zambia 1972

A warm breeze swept up from the Barotze floodplain and wafted through the deserted school laboratory. Through the windows, I could hear the whoops and cries of the students as they played outside in the schoolyard. Friday, last class over; they headed off for the weekend as I surveyed the mess of laboratory equipment they had left behind. I'd blown it again. I couldn't manage 5B double chemistry or any other class for that matter. I felt depressed and disheartened that I was a failure as a teacher.

It was September 1972, and I had just arrived in Zambia, on a two-year teaching contract, fresh from the H.Dip year. All the sociology, philosophy, psychology and history of education I'd studied the previous year wasn't much help when trying to cope with 26 lively African youngsters who could make a mess of my class in ten seconds flat.

As I started to tidy up the debris, I could hear Brother Lawlor in the laboratory next to mine, shuffling about as he too tidied up. He couldn't but have heard the racket that had been going on through the thin partition that divided our rooms. Presently he opened the door, surveyed the scene and said quietly, 'You know Sean, 'tis all in the eye.' I looked up as his eyes made steady contact with mine and learned more about communicating authority in nine seconds than I had in the previous nine months doing 'the Dip'.

As a young teacher, I couldn't understand why it was that when I entered a classroom the students ignored me and continued messing about; yet when other teachers just stood in the doorway, the students would go scurrying to their desks, get out their books and be ready for class. It wasn't that these teachers were particularly big men or of fearsome disposition, they just had it, that 'savoir faire', the knack! I watched and listened as they would quietly, firmly and in low tones change the boisterous class that I had just left into a directed learning forum. They actually succeeded in getting work done!

It took me the next few years to 'serve my time' and to learn the basics about effective communication and classroom management. Experience is a great school, but the fees are very high! After nearly 30 years in the classroom, I'm still learning. I am grateful to those teachers I have been fortunate to meet over the years who helped me with a hint here, a tip there, a friendly comment or a quiet word of encouragement. Why wasn't I taught these basics during my training? It would have saved me so much pain, depression and self-doubt.

Many years later, I resolved to pass on, in a structured way, some of the 'tricks of the trade' that I had learned over the years. Trainee teachers are ill served if they are not shown the basic skills of classroom management. While all teachers have their own individual style depending on personality, age, gender, experience, subject, class group, school ethos, location and other factors, nevertheless there are, as in any skill, basic do's and don'ts. This book is an attempt to provide a distillation of what we have gained from our own experience and learned from our colleagues over the last 30 years teaching full-time in secondary schools.

Good teaching is a complex art. It is not easy to hold the attention of a class of teenagers, to present material which cannot always be exciting, to explain key concepts, while at the same time needing to deal with interruptions, ignore distractions, answer questions, and be constantly alert to the various tricks that students may get up to. It is an emotionally draining task which is not fully understood by the general public who tend to carp about short working days and long holidays.

Not everyone can teach. It requires a certain disposition and personality to work with young people. It also demands the ability to dig deep within oneself from time to time and find the 'steel' to survive, in what can often be a hostile classroom environment. There are elements of teaching that amount to crowd control. Some students can be extraordinarily cruel and many class groups, when presented with a teacher whom they perceive to be weak, vulnerable or a 'soft target', will mercilessly shred that person.

What follows are descriptions of strategies that we find useful in enabling us to create a positive learning environment in our classrooms. The ideas and suggestions in this book are based on our own experience of teaching large classes of urban students, many of whom are disadvantaged.

Please keep in mind that once any skill or technique which can be used in the management of students in classrooms is described in words, it may take on a rigidity that is not intended by the authors. Often it is the tone of teachers' interactions with the students that determines, to a large extent, whether their actions are successful or not. In our interaction with those in our care, we must at all times, be deeply respectful. It is in that spirit that we advance some ideas and strategies aimed at helping teachers in their work.

Different teachers adopt different approaches, either consciously or unconsciously which are particular to themselves. All have 'a way' of doing things. It is important that how we operate is brought strongly into our awareness because it is only then that we can begin to evaluate the effectiveness or otherwise of our behaviours and perhaps also become more mindful of the emotional impact our contact has on the students in our care.

Teaching is such a personal skill, it is unlikely that all the ideas and opinions that follow will meet with total accord within the teaching profession. There is no orthodoxy. There is no one way that's right all the time and in all situations. There are no definitive rules to follow, no magic formulae for managing classes. This is why teaching is such a demanding profession.

Teachers work in isolation in their classrooms and consequently it is not easy to pick up tips or 'tricks of the trade' from others unless we deliberately ask. Even then, the information may not be forthcoming because often teachers themselves have not consciously thought about their skill. This book seeks to answer a question asked by many young teachers beginning their careers: 'How do they do it?'

Sean O'Flynn

Part 1

On becoming a teacher

...the essence of education is becoming, the gradual discovery of what it means to be human, the search for a personal identity, an identity which brings individual autonomy within a community structure.

Ó Suilleabháin (1986)

■ Application and interview

For a new teacher approaching the end of an Initial Teacher Training course the search for a job is usually paramount. The availability of teaching jobs can vary quite considerably, depending on the geographical area, subject area, and even the time of year. Teaching posts are advertised in the national press and on newspaper websites, although many schools advertise in the local press rather than nationally. Education authorities also advertise centrally on a website. Details can be obtained from individual authorities. If a post seems interesting, ask for the application pack. This should include a job description, person specification and information about the school, as well as the application form itself, and can give a clearer idea of the post.

The first step in a successful interview is the completion of the application form (or, in the case of a private post, the preparation of the CV and supporting letter). The person specification should tell you the skills, knowledge and experience you need in order to be called for interview. It is, therefore, important to answer the requirements point by point, in order, stating where you acquired and/or have used your skills, knowledge and experience. Remember that the application form is the medium through which you can give the personnel committee their first impression of you. A clear and ordered form in which you get your message across well will indicate good communication skills and will impress favourably. Although some information is probably best written on the form, larger sections are clearer if typed separately, numbered and securely attached with a 'please see attached sheet x' reference in the appropriate place.

Most forms include sections for other relevant experience and interests and your reasons for wanting the job. This is where you can impress by including all that you have to offer over and above your teaching qualifications. Add any qualification, experience or recognition gained in some extracurricular activity from a sporting, cultural or philanthropic organisation. Examples might include: having a diploma in drama, first aid or music, work experience pertaining to young people such as a youth club, sporting or scouting organisation or adventure centre. Also mention any extra subjects which you are qualified and willing to teach.

These might include subjects such as Religion, Citizenship, PSHE, Relationships and Sexuality, Media Studies, Substance Abuse, Environmental Studies and Information Technology. Remember to put down all your interests, hobbies and sporting activities, and the extracurricular activities such as drama, games, chess club or debating you would be willing to undertake if offered a position at the school. There is always an expectation that any young teacher joining a school will bring new energy and enthusiasm to the teaching staff. In your reasons for wanting the job it can be helpful to point out how committed you are to teaching in general and to the ethos of the school in particular, (having gleaned this from the school's mission statement in the application pack). If you can, indicate how your skills and interests are of value to the school.

Interview panels can vary considerably in size and formality. They can include the Head teacher and deputy, the chair of governors, a parent governor, a teaching governor representative, the head of department and other governors on the personnel subcommittee. In line with equal opportunities legislation, all candidates should be asked the same questions, although follow-up questions for clarification can be added.

Do's and Don'ts at interviews

Do find out beforehand as much as you can about the school, its ethos and the position that is on offer. If there is an informal visit before the interview, attend if you can. During such a visit you can find out a lot about the department and the school in general; you can get a sense of the place and how well you might fit in and enjoy it there.

Do dress neatly and as formally as you can afford.

Do answer every question fully. Don't stop until interrupted by the next question.

Do address the questioner and look them squarely in the eye.

Do demonstrate a willingness to do anything. Indicate what other subjects (other than the ones advertised) you would be willing to teach and what extracurricular activities you would participate in.

Do prepare one or two non-threatening questions about the department, the school in general or future developments. While a school is unlikely to want someone who will 'rock the boat', they may well favour a candidate who is concerned with improving practice.

Do prepare beforehand what you want to get over about yourself. If you have been unable to say all this when answering the set questions, there is usually time at the end when you are asked if there is anything else you would like to add. Then you can do so, briefly.

Do convey the impression that you are a responsible individual capable of conducting yourself in the role that is expected of a teacher at that school.

The trouble with interviews is that you can never be sure if you are 'giving a brilliant shot' or 'shooting yourself in the foot'. So if you have to think on your feet, take a chance, be honest, and go for it.

More schools are now asking candidates to teach a lesson, or part of one, in addition to having an interview. Being observed in these situations can be nerve-racking and it is good for confidence to know you have prepared and planned thoroughly. Reading some of the earlier sections of this book may be useful. Remain as calm as you can; remembering to breathe in a relaxed way can help with this.

One of the first lessons a young teacher learns when looking for a teaching post is that interviews are not always fair. They are often a matter of chance. If you are not successful use it as a learning experience and ask for feedback: what would you need to do differently in order to be successful another time? This can be extremely helpful for future interviews. It can also sometimes be the case that the school liked you but there just happened to be a stronger candidate. Knowing this you might wish to reapply to the same school if another post came up.

As a new teacher having jumped through the hoops of the interview process and having secured a teaching position, you now have to prepare for the task of getting to grips with the realities of teaching.

▨ New to the school

A newly appointed or supply teacher shares with the student teacher the difficult task of getting established in their new school. The 'settling in' period of the first term can be difficult as the teacher strives to get to know the students, the staff and the general ethos of the school.

Before the term begins, the new teacher should obtain a copy of the school rules and discipline procedure, in order to become fully familiar with the system that operates in the school. It is also worth spending some time getting to know the internal layout of the school building, so that when term begins the teacher will know where her classrooms are without having to ask the students.

Where possible, it is useful to meet the teacher you are replacing in order to get information on the classes you will be taking, e.g. profile of each student, course material covered to date, textbook being used, and the general standard to expect. It is also an advantage to meet beforehand with a member of the staff, preferably from the same department, who would introduce you to the staff on the first day and help you to get a locker or some base in the staffroom so that you won't feel too lost during the first week. Modern secondary schools with large busy staffs can be lonely places for the newcomer, so it is advisable to plan and anticipate both your needs and concerns. Above all, don't be afraid to ask for help. Established teachers are only too willing to help the newcomer, but they need to be invited to do so.

▨ Initial class contact

The tone teachers establish on first contact with a new class is critical. Teachers, if they are to survive, must define the class dynamic in their own terms at once, and show students that they are capable of getting them to respond to the teacher, and not the other way round.

A mistake many teachers make on the first occasion they meet a new class is to be too friendly and familiar with the students. One teacher recalls pushing through the door of a classroom in his first school and walking towards the teacher's desk.

> *'I was new to the school and this was my first contact with the notorious 8B. As I placed my books on the desk, a boy in the front row smiled and I returned the smile. The boy continued to smile and asked a question.*
>
> *"Are you our new maths teacher, Sir?"*
>
> *'That's right, I replied and continued to smile.*
>
> *'Another boy asked "Are you strict Sir, like Mr Murphy was?"*
>
> *'I looked towards the second student, took a breath to answer, but before I could respond a third student called from the back of the room. "Mr Murphy was a spacer!"*
>
> *'The class exploded with ribald laughter. I was no longer smiling, I tried to redeem the situation, but it was too late. In fifteen seconds, I had lost a lot of ground with this new class.'*

This example may seem trivial, but if this pattern of interaction were to continue, this teacher would have found it difficult to retain any control over Class 8B. The students had taken the initiative and were beginning to control him. He was too friendly and forthcoming at the beginning and had learned the wisdom of the old adage given to new teachers; don't smile 'til Christmas.

A new teacher may be nervous on the first day so it is helpful to have a plan of action worked out beforehand, in order to take the initiative and keep it. Some of the following suggestions may be helpful.

> *Introduce yourself immediately in a formal way, e.g. 'My name is Mr O'Flynn and I will be your maths teacher for the coming year.' Write your name (as you would like to be addressed) on the board.*

Follow straight away with an instruction asking the students to take out their timetables. Check that the students' timetable corresponds with that of the teacher both in time and in location. Do this slowly. This exercise occupies the students straight away and diverts the focus of attention away from the teacher.

To 'break the ice' and to keep the momentum going check the class list for any unrecorded omissions or additions. Do not rush. Take your time. Call out each name and when the student answers 'present', look at the student, before calling the next name. Ask any student who tries to be smart (and there will be at least one!) to stand and repeat the comment. Say nothing but leave the student standing and continue to check the rest of the class list before returning to and telling the 'comedian' to sit down. These little incidents afford the teacher an opportunity to meet the students in her class and to establish herself as the one who is in charge.

The first lesson is an appropriate time for the teacher to issue her own class rules. The following are an example of class rules used in one school:

1. Enter and leave the classroom in a quiet and orderly fashion.

2. Sit at your assigned desk and take out your diary and all other class requirements.

3. Allow other students to work without interruption or distraction.

4. Raise your hand and wait quietly for your teacher's attention if you have a question or comment.

5. Do all work to the best of your ability.

The teacher could explain the reasoning behind these rules and encourage a discussion leading to an agreement with the whole class group that they are fair and reasonable. The teacher can then write the rules on the board and ask the students to copy them into their diaries. Agree on how you and they wish to be addressed.

Many teachers with senior classes take the opportunity during the first day back to discuss with the class their plan of work for the first term or for the year. Students like to have some idea of the order of events, to know when they are likely to be finished and what is expected of them.

These are just some suggestions as to what new teachers can do to ease themselves into a relationship with a new class on the first day of school in September. The important thing is that the teacher has a plan for his first contact with a new class. Classroom management problems rarely arise on the first day. The students will only be 'sussing out' the new teacher and will be busy establishing or re-establishing their own 'pecking order' within the class.

Experienced teachers have to do exactly the same things to establish themselves as people deserving of respect. They have to lay down ground rules that will operate in their classes and set the stage for the year's work. Time spent doing this is time well spent.

■ The start-up routine

Most teachers have a set way of beginning their classes. The start-up routine a teacher uses will depend on whether the students are already in the room and the teacher comes to them or the class comes to the teacher in his own room. It also depends on the personality of the teacher, the age of the students, their level of maturity and general behaviour. How one would approach a senior class is totally different from the way one would interact with a group of younger students.

Some teachers when they meet an enthusiastic bunch of Year 7 students (as they come running down the corridor) do not allow them to enter the classroom until they have lined up in pairs, by the wall at the door. 'Pairs means in twos, not groups.' Any student pushing is sent 'back to the end of the line'. The students stand by the door and wait until the teacher indicates to them that they are to enter the classroom – 'Slowly – no pushing'. The teacher insists that students go to their allocated places (see below), instead of rushing down to the seats at the back of the class. The teacher surveys each student as they enter, checking their appearance and uniform. Any student who misbehaves is asked to step aside until the class has entered. Then finally the teacher deals with the students she has kept back by asserting her authority, 'Take your jacket off please', 'Straighten your uniform', 'Where's your tie?', 'Don't push.'

This routine may seem unnecessarily draconian to those not in day-to-day contact with boisterous teenagers. However, it is a useful strategy to employ, especially with junior classes, to ensure that an orderly atmosphere and a respectful tone are established even before the lesson begins. It makes the teacher's presence 'felt' and demonstrates that the teacher is in charge.

If an individual student or class group is going to challenge you or resist your efforts to work with them, it is as well to find that out early on. It is best to establish your authority in a forum where your instructions are simple, clear, reasonable and consequently unchallengable. Once you are successful at that level you can move to being positive and thus begin to create a positive working atmosphere in the room. Failure to assert your authority immediately may lead to a negative questioning attitude arising in the student group and this may develop into deeper resistance.

The same dynamic applies for example to refereeing a football game. On the day of the big game, the referee has to establish himself first as the most reasonable person on the field and then as the most unreasonable when players break the rules. A referee who is hesitant about telling players to stand back the required distance for a free kick, who is indecisive about making decisions, unsure of the rules and unwilling to send off players who have committed a particular foul, will not put his 'stamp' on the game. Teachers similarly need to put their 'stamp' on the class.

If the class is already in the classroom before the teacher, the routine is slightly different but the implied message is the same, i.e. a new lesson is about to begin and a new teacher is taking over. Some teachers will alter the physical environment of the classroom as a practical demonstration of this assertion of their legitimacy and authority. For example, if the lights are on when the teacher enters the room he may turn them off and vice versa. The teacher may ask a student to open the window, and if the room is stuffy he may leave the door open until the stale air has been vented and the 'hot house atmosphere' has been replaced by cooler fresh air. A stuffy atmosphere can contribute significantly to class restlessness, especially if the class has been in the same room for some time. A change of air can have a calming influence on a class group and so help to reduce the context for misbehaviour.

Some teachers, on entering the room, ask the students to stand at their desks while they get out their textbooks, exercise books, diaries, etc., and only permit the class to take their seats when all the students are ready to start working. This has the merit of reducing the chaos and disruption at change of class and reduces potential opportunities for students to delay and disrupt the teaching. As soon as the class sits down it is essential that they are given work to do straight away, otherwise the initiative gained by such an ordered beginning is lost.

Some teachers have their own unique way of starting a lesson. One teacher explains her routine as follows:

'Having placed my books and class file on the teacher's desk I walk around the classroom. There are a number of reasons for this. I try to make contact with the students individually, inquiring as to who is absent today, how students who have been sick or bereaved are faring. I congratulate students who have been involved in sporting or extracurricular activities. I am also engaged in establishing my territorial control over the whole room. I ask that jackets and bags are removed from the desks, that any empty chairs be placed under the tables, that the alignment of the tables be straightened, that students get their books out and opened at the appropriate page, that homework be displayed, and that schoolbags be removed from the aisles. I do not entertain any requests to go to the toilet or lockers at

this time. When I'm back at the teacher's desk, I announce the objective of that day's lesson and the page of the textbook involved. I clean the board and write in the top left-hand corner: the date, the title of the lesson, and the page.

I open my class file and ask to see a random sample of homework, if assigned in the previous lesson. Finally, I call on a named student to recall for the class what had been done during the previous lesson, and where we had stopped at the end of the last class period. I may have to prompt in this recall and revision process as I call the class to order.'

Such a start-up routine establishes the control and legitimacy of the teachers. It communicates their authority. It focuses the students on the task in hand and formally announces the beginning of the lesson. The fact that it is consistent and predictable is beneficial to all concerned, and it only takes two to three minutes to execute when the routine is established, expected and understood.

Allocation of places

Other teachers use the allocation of places as a method of helping to assert their authority over the students.

'At the beginning of a new school year, after a week or so when I've got to know the students in a new class, I allocate each one to a particular place in my classroom. I place boisterous, attention-seeking students up front where they will receive the notice they seek. I place reliable, conscientious students down the back. I put moody, quiet, withdrawn students by the window. They need the light! Where possible I put gifted and weak students together in order to encourage cooperation and team spirit. Having arranged the students to my satisfaction, I draw a map of the room in my file and note the places allocated to each student. I expect all students to be

seated in their allocated place when I enter the classroom and regard it as a breach of discipline if any are not. I change this arrangement during the term in the light of experience or because of a considered request from a student. Troublesome students usually demand more attention and personal contact. Seating them in the front row allows me to provide this attention without detracting from my focus on the class as a whole. I may involve such students in tasks such as bringing absence notes to the office, getting pens, or wiping the board. While these errands may relieve their natural restlessness, the main objective from my point of view, is to establish communication and to build a relationship with them.'

Other teachers will isolate troublesome students within the classroom.

'I try to keep "ringleaders" apart, either alone or with the conscientious students down the back. The aim is to deprive them of their clique of subservient followers, without whom they are less vociferous.'

Knowing the names

All teachers agree that knowing the first name of each student is an essential prerequisite in gaining any control over the communication in the classroom. Some teachers get the students to display their first names, in large print, on a folded page, for the first week or so. This, combined with the map of the seating arrangement in the classroom, will enable the teacher to learn and remember the students' names.

Whenever a teacher calls a class to order there will always be a few students who ignore what is happening. Attempts by the teacher to establish order using general statements, such as 'Silence please' or 'Pay attention here', have little effect. Students are inclined to treat such injunctions as applying to others but not to themselves. It is more effective to give a *specific instruction to a named student* whom you wish to call to order. Try to offer a positive alternative behaviour with your desist statement. For example, 'Michael, stop talking, now, and read the second paragraph on page 14 please', is much more effective than bleating 'Quiet please'. The use of the first name is significant here. It focuses attention on the individual concerned. By using their first names, the teacher conveys to the students that she 'knows' them and that she is 'on the ball'. Conversely, forgetting students' names will be interpreted by students as a sign that the teacher is incompetent, and may give the impression that she is 'a bit spaced out' and consequently an easy target for a laugh.

Desperate measures!

There will be occasions when despite a teacher's best efforts the class is still unsettled and noisy. On such occasions, some teachers resort to the use of dictation! Though of limited educational value, dictation can be quite effective at getting a class to calm down. It has the distinct advantage of requiring the students to get themselves organised with a pen, an exercise book, and a ruler, evinced by such questions as, 'Can I write in red, Sir? Must we start on a new page? Do I rule the margin?', etc. All this activity directs the focus of the class on the teacher and what is being dictated, as heads go down to transcribe the piece. The teacher might use short sentences or phrases, repeated twice, and spell 'hard' words, as required. If necessary with a weak class, he may need to write the note on the board and get the students to copy it down, neatly. A short passage is sufficient, as the purpose of the exercise is merely to help settle things down, create a calm atmosphere in the room and allow the teacher to gain sufficient control to begin teaching. A similar effect can be achieved with a 'good' class by launching directly into the work but this is likely to prove disastrous with weaker students.

Once good quality attention has been achieved, the teacher can begin to teach the lesson.

■ **Timing the lesson**

A short recap of the previous lesson, to put this one in context, is followed by a formal introduction to new material. This 'listening time' requires near total silence and absolute attention on the part of the students. The time required will vary considerably from class to class. It depends on the subject matter under consideration, as well as the age, level of ability and maturity of the students. It can range from between three to fifteen minutes.

As the teacher teaches the lesson, she scans the class for any signs of mischief or indications that a student is about to disturb others. Teachers also watch for signs of inattention and day-dreaming. No matter how dazzling the teacher's presentation may be, the students' minds can often be a 'thousand miles away'. Students therefore need to be 'brought into the room', and helped to be fully present before they can begin to learn. This 'grounding' of the student in the here and now is an essential element of effective teaching.

The techniques employed by teachers in classroom control are expressions of their personality. Whatever your style is going to be, you can learn by observing how others work and develop a way that is effective and comfortable for you. For example, one idea teachers use when they notice a student about to cause disruption, or a student not paying attention, is to drop the student's first name into a sentence ,.....pause ,..... and continue once the student has responded and is paying full attention to the lesson, e.g. 'The causes of the Reformation were.....Andrew.....the state of the Church .....etc.'. Another effective idea is to pause in mid-sentence, stare fixedly at the culprit and then having gained her attention to slowly resume the sentence with just a subtle hint of menace or humour in the teacher's tone of voice. No reference is made to any alleged misbehaviour; the teacher simply continues the lesson without interruption. In this way, the teacher can avoid any rancour and unnecessary entanglements with students, while at the same time keeping the class on task, and maintaining a smooth flow of instruction.

After this initial period of concentrated active teaching (during which the students are required to listen and pay close attention to the material), the teacher can ask questions of them to check if they understand the material, and then give the students written work to do based on what has just been taught. For example, in maths, following an explanation of a particular technique or principle, the teacher asks the students to try, on their own, a number of questions/problems/exercises, similar to the example that has just been demonstrated.

During this working period of approximately ten to fifteen minutes, the students can work quietly either alone or in small groups. A certain amount of low level conversation will be inevitable and tolerated as the students get organised to do their work. The focus of classwork moves from the teacher to the students. This allows the teacher to regain her composure if the lesson has been difficult, take stock of the situation, review the progress of the lesson in terms of time, plan ahead, answer questions as they arise, or help individual students who may be experiencing difficulties. During this period of classwork the more able students, once they have completed their assignment, can be encouraged to help their neighbour overcome any difficulties encountered, or be given further, more advanced, work to do.

The lesson can thus proceed, alternating the pace and focus as the situation demands. The last five minutes of the lesson is also a 'listening time', in which the teacher sums up the lesson, puts it in context with the next lesson and allocates homework if appropriate.

For some subjects like English, this kind of 'choppy' lesson structure does not always suit. Sometimes it is best to put all the exercises, answers and corrections to one side, focus on the play or story involved, and let the piece of literature weave its own magic.

Whatever structure a teacher chooses for her lesson, the aim is to seek a sense of smooth ordered progress in which the teacher knows exactly where the class is going, and the students feel that some progress is being made. The net effect of this is that students feel safe and looked after in that teacher's care.

■ Asking and taking questions

The root of the word education comes from the Latin 'educo': to lead out. Ideally, good teaching is a series of structured questions, that lead the students by degrees to discover new knowledge based on their own experience. So the theory goes. In practice, however, a lot of 'induco', i.e. the provision and assimilation of information, goes on in schools, where questioning is reduced to checking that the material covered has been understood and learned.

Teaching, by the questioning technique, is a process whereby the students discover answers and arrive at conclusions, having followed a process of reasoning of their own. Students can then begin to share in the excitement of discovery and the joy of real learning. Questioning is a skill acquired through practice. It can best be learned by watching a master teacher in action. New teachers should seek every opportunity to watch experienced teachers operating in class and to note how, by using crafted questions, they motivate students to think creatively and contribute to class discussion.

The teacher starts by exploring the 'known' experience/ knowledge of the students, raises their awareness/curiosity and develops the topic from there. Unless students have the 'hook of awareness and wonder' on which to focus their attention, any information, no matter how interesting it may be to the teacher, becomes just something else that 'floats by' the students' consciousness and is quickly forgotten. The ability to ground the topic in a practical problem, or known experience of students is the first part of mastering this technique of teaching by questioning. Questions like 'Have you ever seen.....?, Have you ever felt like.....?, Did you ever wonder about.....?, Can you imagine what it would be like to.....?, Did you ever hear of someone who....?' help to raise the issue and to get a discussion going. Every student can answer these questions and some 'weak' students may indeed have much to offer from their own personal experience.

Teachers introduce a new topic by addressing easy questions to named students and as the topic develops address more difficult questions to the class in general. They try to make the questions open-ended with many possible correct answers. If incorrect answers are given they rephrase the question or pick the least incorrect answer 'You are very close' and follow through with more questions leading to valid conclusions.

Many teachers, when asking or taking questions in large junior classes, insist that students raise their hands to avoid the confusion of many answers being offered at the same time. If many hands are raised the teacher can go from left to right across the room inviting responses or questions. This inculcates in students the discipline of 'waiting one's turn' and listening to another student's answer or point of view.

When addressing easy questions to energetic students in younger classes the teacher can name the student first before asking the question. 'Paul, ...what is the .....?' This avoids the difficulty of getting 'drowned' in a 'sea' of raised hands of students crying 'Sir, Sir, Sir.....', making it difficult for the teacher to discern any replies in the enthusiastic verbal melee.

Some readers may feel that addressing questions to specific students may cause embarrassment if they do not know the answer. This can be avoided by reassuring students that we learn by our mistakes, and if we do not make any we will not learn. The teacher can create an atmosphere where it is perfectly acceptable to make mistakes. This may involve reprimanding any sniggering when particularly daft answers are given. Emphasis should be placed on the importance of respecting the participation of every student in class discussion and in encouraging all contributions. Shy, withdrawn students can be encouraged to become fully involved so that the discussion is not confined to extrovert or 'bright' students. Teachers commend and praise particularly intelligent or insightful questions or responses. 'Well done, Mary, that is an excellent question to ask. Did you all hear that? Mary wants to know why .....'. In the case of more difficult questions or with the more lethargic senior students the teacher addresses the questions to the whole class. She then listens to all the answers offered; acknowledges, corrects or comments on all contributions; and follows through on the more promising replies.

The sensitivity of the teacher is an important factor in this approach. When done well, the result can be inspirational. Conversely, when done ineffectively, there is no faster route to chaos and confusion. That said, teaching using the questioning technique has benefits both for student motivation, and for the teacher in building a relationship with the class.

■ Making announcements and giving instructions

Teachers frequently require a class to do something specific and need to issue clear, concise instructions as to what it is they require. In order to do this the class must be silent – totally quiet and receptive. Some physical gesture or signal is useful when establishing order and gaining attention. Teachers often do things like clap hands, use pauses, name noisy students and call them to order, use facial expressions, or maintain eye contact, to get a class to settle down and listen.

The manner and tone of delivery are important. The teacher has to avoid being too stern and imperious on the one hand, and too diffident and unconvincing on the other. The manner of the delivery ought to have, to use Marland's (2002) term, a 'warm firmness' about it. The voice issuing the command should be strong, decisive, and warm. If the teacher uses an overly aggressive tone, it may well set the context for later loud or cheeky exchanges or indeed subversive behaviours by the students.

It is better if the teacher phrases all instructions in a positive manner, e.g. 'Be early' rather than 'Don't be late', 'Leave the room tidy', rather than 'Don't leave the room in a mess.' The former emphasises a standard, while the latter is often perceived as a criticism.

Care must also be taken to avoid framing an instruction in the form of a question. 'Put your hand up if you require a ruler' is better than 'Does anyone need a ruler?'

When giving instructions, in particular to Years 7 and 8, a teacher may find that the students on hearing the first part of the instruction begin to move, resulting in the later part of the instruction being ignored in the ensuing confusion. Therefore, it is suggested that the teacher preface any announcement with the caveat, 'Nobody is to move until I have finished'. Avoid, if possible, giving a second instruction until the first one has been obeyed. All instructions must be clear, without doubt or ambiguity, and should be repeated.

When issuing instructions to young students it is very likely that a teacher could easily be misunderstood. Therefore, some teachers, having finished making an announcement to a class, ask a student to repeat the instruction to ensure that it was understood completely: 'Frank, would you repeat what you heard me say just now so that everybody is clear on what we have to do?'.

Often, teachers themselves cause confusion by their manner of delivery when making announcements. The following is an example of how not to issue an instruction. A teacher says to a Year 7 class, 'Take out your geography books. Open page 49 and begin answering questions 1 to 7. Read each question carefully before you attempt to answer them. Write a short paragraph on each. You have about twenty minutes to do it, so that means you have just less than three minutes for each question. OK? Any questions? No? You can start now and no talking.'

Not surprisingly, a great deal of frustrated confusion would follow such an announcement. The chaos starts with repetitive questions such as: 'What page? How many questions must we do? What questions? Can I go to the toilet? My pen's run out! What page? How many lines must I write? How long is a paragraph? What did he say? What page? What time is it? How long have we got? Is it on page 20?' The reason for the blizzard of repetitive questions is because each student is only concerned with the difficulty he is experiencing at that moment, and does not hear the answers the teacher is giving to other students. The troublemakers in the class will be quick to exploit this type of situation to 'have a laugh' and in the confusion to play up. If there is any room for misunderstanding, confusion and messing about, then that is what will happen.

In this case, with a young class, the teacher would be more effective if he were to issue each instruction independently and pause after each one, to see that it was obeyed before continuing to the next instruction. Alternately, the teacher could write all the factual details of the instruction on the board. Explain to the class what they are required to do. Answer all relevant questions and queries. Hold the attention of the class until it is clear that everyone knows what to do and only then, instruct the students to take out their books.

When actually issuing instructions a teacher should not enter into any discussion as to the reason for the command. To do so beforehand or afterwards is fine, but not whilst in the process of issuing the instruction. Explanations at this point only complicate the issue and introduce an element of doubt or misunderstanding into the process.

It is a good idea to avoid coupling a command with a grievance, e.g. 'Stop scraping the chairs at the back of the room. I am sick and tired of telling you. You do it every time you come into the room.' The whine is wearing, ineffective and distracts from an instruction, which should be clear, precise, and delivered in a measured tone. Whining puts the teacher in the role of 'victim' and places the class in the 'bad' role, which they will resent.

When issuing instructions, a teacher's own expectations are critical, as students will often be more sensitive to what the teacher expects than to what he says. If a teacher creates a positive classroom climate, students will accept instruction and are happy to comply. Students like to know that someone is in charge and knows what is going on. The teacher must at least look like and sound as if he might be that person!

The toilet

Continuous requests by students to go to the toilet can pose a difficulty for an inexperienced teacher. If the teacher accedes to every request, the students will quickly deduce that the teacher is a 'soft touch' and a veritable procession to the toilet will develop. It is also likely that the teacher on entering the classroom each day will be greeted with a rush of such requests. While teachers are anxious to avoid causing genuine discomfort to any student, at the same time, it is necessary to provide some resistance to avoid being 'taken for a ride' and the creation of unnecessary disruption to classes.

It is inadvisable to entertain any requests by students to go to the toilet at the beginning of the lesson. Many teachers defer these requests until the class is settled and the lesson has begun. 'Ask me again in five minutes time.' If the case is genuine the student will ask again and can then be allowed to go. Often the student was just bored and they usually forget to ask a second time. As well as deferring suspect requests, avoid allowing students out immediately before or after a break.

Latecomers

An issue that can cause difficulty for some teachers is how to deal with students arriving late for class. Most teachers expect latecomers to knock on the door before entering the classroom and approach the teacher, to offer an explanation as to why they are late, either verbally

or with a note from their parents. If the student's late arrival is not a regular occurrence then teachers ought to be sympathetic, welcome the student to the class, assure them that they are fine, indicate non-verbally acceptance of the excuse offered, fill them in on where the class is at in the lesson, and urge them to 'fall in' as quickly as they can. The teacher's main concern is to keep the lesson flowing smoothly and not to allow the arrival of a latecomer to disrupt the proceedings. We have all been late occasionally for appointments and arrive rushed and flustered. On such occasions, the last thing we need is a harangue or blaming from a superior. In the same way most students feel uncomfortable and exposed when they arrive late for class and do not need a reprimand from the teacher.

There will, of course, always be the few students who are chronic latecomers. The main issue for the teacher is not to let the arrival of latecomers disrupt the flow of the lesson. The strategy most teachers use with such students is to defer action: 'See me later after class'. When the lesson is over, the teacher can listen to the explanation offered, point out the number of times the student has been late recently and state clearly that late arrival for class will no longer be accepted. The teacher may assist the student in devising a plan to avoid future lateness, but will press for a commitment from the student to change. Despite a teacher's best efforts, however, there will always be the recalcitrant individual who will push the boundaries of reasonableness, continue the habit of coming in late, and with whom the teacher has to resort to the school discipline system to effect a change in behaviour.

In any discussion with a student on the reason for their lateness, one should be aware of the possibility that the student may be unwilling to reveal the real reason for his lateness. Teachers must look for hidden reasons for lateness, before jumping to the conclusion that the student is lazy.

▦ Pacing

The pace of instruction is critical. If it is too slow, the more able students become bored. Too fast a pace, on the other hand, results in the 'weaker' students becoming frustrated. When the intellectual needs of students are not being met by the content or process of a lesson, they will seek satisfaction through other avenues such as messing about or having a laugh.

The transition by a young teacher, from the academic demands of a university college course, to teaching junior classes in a secondary school, is considerable. Such a change requires an awareness of the need to slow down and tune in to the actual capabilities of the students. Young teachers at the beginning of their careers often overestimate the ability of their students and try to cover too much material, too quickly. It is often a teacher's way of coping with insecurity and nervousness. By setting a cracking pace, the teacher hopes that the work rate will keep the students so busy that they won't get up to any misbehaviour. This tactic is totally counter-productive. Piling on too much work, without any regard to the students' ability to absorb the new material, can often lead to frustration, which in turn will lead to incidents of indiscipline. It is much more satisfactory for all concerned to do a little well so that success is assured.

The capabilities of students vary enormously with age and ability. 'There are horses for courses.' Often, in a school that streams the student intake, the difference in ability between the 'top' and 'weakest' classes in a particular year group can be greater than the difference between some Year 7 and some Year 11 classes! The teacher's job, therefore, is to find a baseline of ability and knowledge within the class. This may require considerable testing and a return to basics before going on to present new material. It is important that all new material be presented at a suitable pace so that the students 'can do' what is required of them and experience success in their learning.

Allowance must also be made for the time of day, the day of the week and the time of the year. Teaching maths, second period, on a cold wet Tuesday morning in November, is a totally different experience from teaching the same lesson last period on a fine, sunny Friday afternoon in May. Do not expect to get much done on the last day of term, last period on a Friday, or when there is any disruption to the school routine that will have the students distracted.

■ Tests

It is often difficult for teachers to know how much of what they have taught has been understood, or how much new knowledge their students assimilate. In normal class teaching, finding the answers to these questions is a haphazard business. A few pupils answering questions correctly can give the false impression that everyone understands the material. It is not until teachers look at pupils' written answers to a test that they will discover how much of their cherished exposition went 'over the heads' of many of the students. Experienced teachers who are really tuned into their students can sense when they are 'gone'. The eyes have a vacant, 'not at home' look. The only reliable way to gauge the effectiveness of one's teaching is to administer a series of short tests. The correcting is tedious but the feedback will ensure that the teacher stays reasonably close to the reality of the students' capabilities.

■ Tools of the trade

The board

Despite all the innovations in educational audio-visual aids, 'chalk and talk', or 'marker and talk', as it is now, are still the basic fundamental tools of the trade. The board is a visual medium where clarity is all important. The presentation on the board must be ordered in sequence. A jumble of writing will only confuse students.

As mentioned earlier, many teachers, at the beginning of a lesson, wipe the board completely clean; they write the date, the topic and the page number of the textbook on the top left-hand corner. Then they divide the board into two sections. As the lesson proceeds, they work down the left-hand side before continuing on to the top of the right-hand side.

It takes practice to master the knack of writing clearly and legibly in straight lines on the board.

- ■ The use of different colours helps.

- ■ The height of the letters is usually about two inches.

- ■ Drawing a box around a sentence or a word is the most effective way of highlighting it.

By working in this way, teachers model clarity and order in their work. A board full of disorganised words, without pattern or purpose, will only produce frustration and confusion. While it is true that some very successful teachers are notorious for the chaotic nature of their board presentation, it is equally true that their students perform in spite of this and not because of it.

When using software graphic programs the same point applies. Often a gimmicky presentation can detract from the main focus of the lesson and leave the students wondering 'what was that all about?'

Voice

The teacher's voice is one of the tools of the trade. Without it we cannot work. Like any other tool, it needs minding and care. Just as we tend to take good health for granted, we do not give much consideration to our voice until we, or one of our colleagues, experience a problem with it.

Some teachers find that every September, at the beginning of the school year, they get a sore throat, which can last for weeks. This is often due to the voice being forced. Teachers project their voices to gain control over certain classes. The raising of one's voice to a constant high pitch not only puts a strain on the vocal chords but is also a self-defeating exercise. All classes have a residual murmur, the level of which will be influenced by the pitch and strength of the teacher's own voice. If the teacher's voice is low and soft, then the class murmur tends to remain low, but if the teacher's voice is high-pitched and forceful, then the students are inclined to compensate by unconsciously raising the level of the class murmur. Teachers therefore try to keep their voices soft and gentle for normal working. This has a calming effect on the students and is conducive to creating a good working atmosphere. It also has the advantage that on those occasions when teachers do have to raise their voices, to make a point or to reprimand a student, it will have a greater effect.

There are certain mannerisms that teachers need to be aware of. Every school, for example, has a teacher who goes on and on in a high-pitched monotone whine. If you happen to visit that class you will notice that the students have a glazed look in their eyes and look as if they are completely turned off. How else could they survive? Another mannerism to be aware of is that of not finishing your... sentences! We all know of a...? teacher, who always raises their voice in the tone of a…? question. This is an attempt to get students to pay attention and follow a line of thought. However, it can just as easily produce sheepish repetitive answering without the students engaging their brains.

Posture and clothes

Posture

The way teachers hold themselves can demonstrate a lot about their character to a class of students. They glean information about their teachers just by observing their posture and body language. It helps, when in front of a class, to be as relaxed as possible and avoid being hunched up at the teacher's desk or behind a textbook, as if hiding. Many teachers are conscious of their posture and deliberately walk tall to project a formal, professional image.

Clothes

The way teachers dress also conveys messages about how they feel about themselves and what they are doing. It has an impact on the students. It is best to wear clothes that you feel confident in and that honestly express your sense of status and self. Casual or fashion clothes may be fine but, as in other aspects of teaching, it is best to be slightly conservative and dress for the role which you aspire to. Formality in dress (whether we like it or not) does convey authority and competence to impressionable children and helps to project an image of the teacher as one who is organised and professional.

■ 'With-it-ness'

This is a term coined by Kounin (1977) which conveys that a teacher is fully aware of what is going on in the class and is clearly nobody's fool; it demonstrates presence of mind. A teacher displaying 'with-it-ness' can recognise the initial signs of any messing about as soon as it begins; can detect quickly any indication of bullying, mocking or whispering among the students; is alert to attempts by students to pass notes to one another in class; can recognise homework that has been copied, or forged signatures on notes purporting to come from parents, and is alert to students who skip classes or 'duck out' of school. The with-it teacher will also remember what the class was doing at the end of the last lesson, what text was used and which students need to be checked as a consequence of things that happened, or failed to happen, during the previous lesson. In short, a 'with-it' teacher is one who is aware, alive, alert and 'out there'. With-it-ness involves being aware of what time and what day it is. On a Friday, do not promise to collect the homework tomorrow.

The notion of with-it-ness can be extended to include a general knowledge of what constitutes current teenage culture. This might involve occasionally watching television channels such as MTV, *Kerrang!*, or programmes such as *The Simpsons* or one of the soaps such as *EastEnders* in order to be familiar with current music, film, fashion, football and sporting events.

◾ Homework

Different schools put a varying emphasis on homework. Some schools and some parents seem to use it as an index of a teacher's competence. This value judgement could be made in ignorance of the fact that the same teacher might be an insecure individual, who maintains order in class through domination and fear. While students may work very hard at that subject because of the threat of punishment, it might also be the case, that as a result, subjects taught by more humane and reasonable teachers are not accorded the same importance in the eyes of the students or parents.

It is difficult to offer any definitive guidelines on homework. It varies from subject to subject and depends on such factors as the ability of the students, the time of year, the proximity of exams and the school policy and ethos. The purpose of homework can vary. Sometimes teachers wish to check the students' understanding of the material that has been taught in class. At other times teachers may use homework to present tasks that challenge the students' ability or perhaps simply to keep the material fresh in their minds until the next lesson. There always should be a valid educational purpose in giving an assignment. There is no point in giving homework just for the sake of it, as a punishment or from habit. The issuing of homework should take cognisance of the students' ability to complete it. There is no point in giving homework to a class when the majority of the students just cannot do it. When too much homework is given, or if the students are unable to attempt it, it is likely that all of the next lesson will be devoted to going over the previous day's homework and the class stagnates in negativity.

Some teachers set homework regardless of what other homework has been assigned by other teachers that day. Students will always protest that they have been given too much to do. However, a glance at a student's diary will show if that is the case. In many schools, there is a homework timetable to ensure that some sense of fair play prevails for all concerned. For many students the school day is demanding enough, without being required to spend hours at further study later that evening. For the more able students it is not such a burden. It can provide an opportunity for parents to be involved in what is going on in school and, where necessary, to support their children.

When setting homework, it is wise to make sure that it is of direct relevance to the students' need to do well in that subject. Keep it as short as possible, so that it leads to the minimum of frustration for students. Having set the work, it is only fair that the teacher checks the work; therefore homework should be structured in such a way that it can be easily and quickly corrected. Even in subjects like English and history, where considerable writing is involved, clear paragraphing and the highlighting of quotes can help the students to structure their work and facilitate the teacher in its correction.

■ Files

The keeping of accurate records is vital in any programme of effective classroom management. Some teachers use a large ring binder, which is divided into sections for each of their classes. Each section contains items such as the class list of names, with test results or comments, the seating arrangement, a map of the classroom and a customised diary.

During, and at the end of each lesson, the teacher can note very briefly what material was covered, where the lesson stopped, what homework, if any, was issued and the plan for the next lesson. The daily comment might also include the names of any students who were absent, late, gave trouble, 'forgot' to bring in their homework assignment, were sent out of class or were given a detention.

Efficient keeping of files is a great help in building confidence and enabling the teacher to be organised. Incidents of indiscipline in class often have their origin in students exploiting a teacher's own confusion or forgetfulness. Make it easy on yourself. Keep files. Keep them up to date. By keeping some form of class file, the teacher keeps track of everything and the students quickly realise that this teacher never forgets, anything, ever. This reduces considerably the likelihood of students attempting to hoodwink the teacher.

■ Cover lessons

Depending on staffing levels, a teacher may frequently be expected to cover for an absent colleague and to take a cover lesson. This can often be more difficult than teaching a regular class. The teacher may not know the students. They may be disappointed, especially if they are missing a practical subject or a topic they had been looking forward to, or they may be excited that their usual teacher is absent and may be tempted to 'try it on' with a strange teacher to see how far they can control the situation. The strategies suggested for first contact with a class would also apply to this situation.

Cover work should be set either by the absent teacher or by the department. The type of work set can often cause difficulty since it usually involves a lot of reading and writing. The expectation is, in general, that pupils will sit quietly and work independently for the whole lesson. This is rarely, if ever the case, particularly with classes in KS3. Those with a general or specific learning difficulty will require help or they are likely to disrupt out of boredom, frustration or in order to avoid feelings of failure because of difficulty with the work. Students with emotional or behavioural difficulties will usually find the change from their regular teacher a challenge and may disrupt as a result.

Faced with a cover lesson some teachers set the class working with a brief explanation of the task before getting down to their own marking or preparation. This can be fraught with difficulties for the reasons outlined above. Another option is to actively teach the lesson, although this can also be difficult with no time to prepare and, very often, without special knowledge of the subject. However, this approach does make it possible to give more help to those who require it, whilst also offering the 'carrot' of a puzzle or quiz to those who finish enough work well. Such a change in activity is usually welcome, especially in a 50- or 60-minute period. There are many good quality educational puzzle books available which contain plenty of ideas that should keep most students occupied for some time. Some teachers keep a stock of educational videos for just such occasions. It is worth putting effort into making cover lessons as successful as possible, partly for your own confidence, but also to help build relationships with the students: after all, you may be teaching them next year!

■ Staff meetings

Very often, the first contact a new teacher will have with the teaching staff of a school is when they are introduced and welcomed to the school by the head during the September staff meeting. All the new teacher has to do is smile faintly and nod. Do not say anything until you find your feet. In fact, to say anything significant is neither expected nor appreciated. In time, the new teacher will begin to realise that staff meetings in many schools are not meetings as such; they are announcement sessions during which the head informs the staff of decisions already taken.

Many teachers experience staff meetings as generally depressing, demotivating affairs. Notions about collegiality, shared decision making, a middle management tier, whole-school planning, consultation with teaching staff, etc., are laudable concepts that can sometimes bear little or no relation to the administration of school management in the real world. There are of course exceptions, but in our experience it is the head teacher, in consultation with his or her inner circle, who makes the decisions. The rest of the teaching staff are informed at staff meetings. Any teacher, who queries decisions or questions how these decisions are to be implemented, can be regarded as being awkward! Silence at staff meetings is often rewarded.

There are more subtle versions of autocratic control, where those in authority exploit the rhetoric of consensus to secure the consent of staff to decisions already taken. This occurs where opportunity for discussion at staff meetings is offered as a mechanism to give a democratic veneer to autocratic management. In schools where teachers are excluded from exercising any real influence on managerial decisions, staff meetings may for some teachers represent no more than 'dictational fiats with legal backing' (Williams 1989).

Because schools are staffed by professionals, there can exist in schools a tension between a bureaucratic type of management, based on position and status within a hierarchical organisation, and an emerging egalitarian authority, which is based on a teacher's ability, qualifications, knowledge and experience. The work that teachers perform within the classroom is highly complex, demanding and discretionary in character, and it calls upon teachers to perform many managerial tasks. Because teachers are not usually included in the processes that set direction and establish parameters for school decision making, the resulting tension between the demands for teacher discretion and administrative coordination, can lead to tacit, ad hoc compromises between the head teacher and the teachers.

▦ The staffroom

Many teachers find staffrooms stressful places. Because of the stop-start nature of the teaching day and the rushed nature of breaks, a staffroom can often be more akin to a busy train station than to a place of rest. The negativity that accompanies the job of giving instructions and keeping order is often offloaded in the staffroom, so that cynicism and complaint frequently dominate the conversation.

Staffrooms can be odd places with strange customs and peculiar ways of doing things that nobody questions. They tend to be territorial places where fixed groups emerge. It is helpful to a new teacher if someone explains something of the set-up and routine of the staffroom at the beginning of the school year. After that, it is best if newcomers are left alone to find their own place in their own way.

New teachers to a school are often surprised to find that there are many divisions among the teachers in a staff. For example, teachers frequently differ in their attitudes towards the way the school is managed and how the school discipline code is operated. Some teachers favour a traditional authoritarian methodology while others prefer a more liberal/psychological approach.

Often there can seem very little team spirit among a staff as a whole. There may be residual bitterness following internal promotions, or after application for threshold or advanced teacher status if some were unsuccessful. The stress engendered by heavy workloads and the difficulty of managing large classes of adolescents can contribute to a strained atmosphere in staffrooms. Tension often rises towards the end of term or when there are additional pressures such as reports to write or, of course, an Ofsted visit. Part of the difficulty is that teachers spend most of their time with students and relatively little with colleagues so there is little opportunity to air differences constructively, talk things through or even have a laugh together.

■ Parents' evenings

It is generally accepted that parents' evenings are a valuable experience for all those involved in a student's education. They allow teachers to take stock of their classes and to seek to develop a clearer and more concrete picture of each individual student's progress in school.

During these and other meetings with parents, teachers gain some insight into the formative background of each student. For example, when the teachers meet Mrs McCarthy, they will invariably get some understanding of why Jason in Class 8C is as he is and, as a consequence, resolve to be more understanding and compassionate towards the boy in future. Parents often use these meetings to inform the teachers of such things as a chronic illness affecting their child, bereavement in the family, early primary school experiences, or learning difficulties. This information enables the teacher to form a more holistic view of the student.

Unfortunately, many parents whom teachers really want to meet never come to these meetings. They may be ashamed of their child's record of misbehaviour at the school or may have real problems getting to the meeting. The majority of the parents who do come are conscientious and cooperative, anxious to do the best they can for their children. They need to be honestly yet tactfully informed as to the progress or otherwise of their children, and assured of the dedication and commitment of the teachers. All information passed at these meetings must of course be treated in the strictest confidence.

Parents' evenings allow parents to see and experience for themselves what particular teachers are like. This completes the student–parent–teacher triangle, and reduces the possibility that the student will try to play one off against the other.

Some teachers, during their first year of teaching, become anxious about these meetings. 'What will I say to the parents of a student who is experiencing difficulties in my class? Can I be honest and tell the parents how it really is? What if they attack me?' It helps if these teachers keep in mind that the opening sentence in the exchange between the teacher and each parent often sets the tone for the conversation that follows. Many teachers have an opening line prepared to initiate the conversation. With parents of Year 7 pupils the opening, 'How is Liam settling into his new school?' conveys the teacher's care and concern. With the parents of students in Year 11 or 13 an enquiry as to their child's plans for next year will usually help to get things going. When opening a conversation with the parents of known troublemakers an enquiry like 'How is Mary treating you at home?' is guaranteed to establish a commonality between the parent and the teacher.

There are some parents who are overly ambitious for the academic success of their children. The content of their discussion with the teachers revolves exclusively around grades, percentage marks, points in exams, or getting into university. Often these parents are pushing their children to compensate for their own frustrated ambitions, regardless of the abilities of their children. It can be difficult to offer any kind of professional advice to these parents. All one can do is to keep a distance, have one's facts correct, offer one's opinion and leave the decisions to the parents and their child.

When attending parents' evenings bring the file for that particular class, complete with test results, and a record of behaviour. It is also helpful to bring a glass of water for all that talking, and a book to read (or books to mark), so that you have something to be doing if nobody is with you. Parents' evenings are hard work.

■ School reports

The school report is another opportunity to let parents know how their children are progressing at school. It can be a tedious and time-consuming exercise trying to write a meaningful comment on each student, especially if there are large classes involved. There is often a temptation to resort to the clichéd, short comments such as 'Fair' or 'Could do better'.

Some teachers find it helpful during the term to reflect from time to time on their students and to note down their impressions. At the end of term when they come to write reports, they have considered comments already made out.

When writing reports, one should not confine one's comments merely to the results of tests, but should broaden the scope of the perspective, to offer a more comprehensive report on the overall progress of the student.

One wit has drawn up the following glossary of comments as an aid to teachers who wish to be oblique in their communication with parents.

What you say	What you really mean
He's very lively.	He is rowdy, loud, and disruptive.
He has a strong personality.	He's a thug and a bully.
He tries very hard.	Thick as a brick.
Could do better.	Lazy, does nothing.
She gets on with her work quietly.	Which one is she?
Independent-minded.	Troublemaker and loudmouth.
Lively sense of humour.	Scatterbrained and unteachable.
Needs to improve in biology.	You can forget your ambition for him to become a doctor.
Trouble concentrating.	He is away with the fairies.

Be sure to fill in all your students' reports. It is so easy, particularly with options and AS and A level courses, to overlook a student because he is in a different tutor group.

▣ Extracurricular activities

Activities such as drama and sport allow students to demonstrate leadership qualities, organisational ability, social skills, courage, talents and capabilities that often do not find expression in the classroom situation, with its emphasis on academic 'head' work.

Any involvement by teachers in school activities outside of the classroom affords them the opportunity to get to know their students better and to improve their understanding of and relationship with them. Time and effort expended in training school teams, rehearsals for musicals, and in activities such as organising chess contests will be rewarded in terms of improved class management and greater job satisfaction. The whole school system gets a lift from these activities.

▣ Educational visits

Day trips

Much of what has been said of extracurricular activities also applies to day trips. By interacting with students in different surroundings and circumstances, teachers can get a more complete picture of the students' personalities and character.

Day trips, such as geographical, historical, art or scientific visits are focused on having educational outcomes. Trips to adventure centres or mountain walks, while not of direct relevance to the curriculum, can be of great benefit in fostering a positive relationship between teachers and their students.

Great care must be taken in the preparation and conduct of these trips. When the cost of the trip has been calculated, it is advisable to add a little extra to the fare in order to cover unforeseen eventualities, e.g. the student who cannot bring in all the money for the trip or the student who has lost all his pocket money up the mountain and will 'die of hunger' if he can't buy a bag of chips on the way home. Always collect the money well in advance. It is a bother collecting it in dribs and drabs for a few days but at least you do not get caught out if a student does not turn up on the day. One teacher we know has a class bank account into which any money left over is lodged, and is available for future activities. The students control this account.

Students need to be given a checklist of what to bring on the day. If the class is going on a mountain walk then they need to bring old clothes, boots (no trainers allowed as they can slip on the mountainside), rainwear and a packed lunch. Teachers usually place a limit on the amount of spending money a student can bring. A letter should be sent home well in advance of the date of the proposed trip, outlining to parents what is planned, and seeking their consent in writing. Pupils cannot attend a day trip without the signed consent of a parent or guardian. Do not under any circumstances go alone. Consult the head of department or a member of the senior management team as to the legal pupil–teacher ratio for the kind of trip you are planning. It is always a risk when a teacher takes a group of students out of the classroom environment and, particularly in these litigious times, a teacher cannot be too careful.

School trips

In recent years there has been a rapid rise in the number of 'educational visits' undertaken by school parties to European cities and places of interest. In the personal experience of the writers, these tours comprise of marathon coach journeys (often overnight), nauseous sea crossings, sleepless nights, and a couple of near misses that nobody talks about afterwards! Murphy's Law applies to these tours. If anything can go wrong…it will, and even if it can't…it might. The possibilities for students messing about and the opportunities that present themselves for this during a school tour are endless. Teachers have to be vigilant at all times, and be aware of, and when necessary be ready to intervene in, the purchases that students make (anything from fireworks and alcohol to pornography and flick knives). Also teachers may be required to

intrude on things like the heavy petting that can develop down at the back of the bus, or the viewing of adult channels that the students will readily find on the TV sets of their continental hotel rooms. Despite the best efforts of the teachers, 'incidents' can easily occur on these tours. When the tour returns home the teachers generally need three days uninterrupted sleep to recover. Not surprisingly, many teachers have reservations as to the merit of these 'educational' visits.

Exchange programmes with European schools

These are a different proposition entirely and most teachers agree that they are well worth participating in. Not only are they valid educational experiences for the students but they are much less demanding on the teachers who accompany the group. All that is required of the teacher is to get the students safely to and from the exchange school and to perform normal pastoral and teaching duties while there. The students are in the care of their respective exchange parents after school hours.

The students have the opportunity to gain a valuable insight into another culture and to improve their language skills. The exchange can also challenge some of the more vivid stereotypical assumptions that students may have of our European neighbours. It is also of benefit to teachers to spend a week or two in a European school, to observe the differences and similarities of the teaching experience in other countries.

Part 2
Communicating authority in the classroom

The 'master teacher' like the storyteller, comedian or magician, conceals the tricks of the trade in the fabric of his work, so they remain in the background. It takes time to see the 'how' element in their work. What is being taught conceals how it is being taught once interest and curiousity have been aroused.

Effective classroom management is essential if teachers are to facilitate teaching and learning in the 'unnatural' setting of a school. It goes against nature to expect healthy, energetic young people to sit quietly at desks for long periods of time. Expecting them to sit passively at desks for 40-, 50- or 60-minute periods, over five hours a day, five days a week, is a recipe for conflict and stress. Some children simply cannot do it. When one considers the diversity of the personalities and backgrounds of all the actors in the classroom arena, added to the different expectations and requirements of teachers and students, it is inevitable that conflict will arise.

What teachers and school authorities regard as student misbehaviour varies quite widely. Behaviour which would be taken as a serious breach of discipline in one school may be routine in another. In some schools, for example, a student who forgets to bring a textbook to school, fails to complete a homework assignment, or presents herself for class not dressed in full uniform is considered to be in serious breach of school discipline. In other schools, such behaviour is tolerated. The school authorities in these schools only respond to more serious issues such as swearing, overt defiance, aggressive behaviour, vandalism of school property or verbal aggression directed at other students or teachers.

Behavioural problems and classroom disruption rarely occur spontaneously, without pretext or cause. Incompetent school management, low morale among the teaching staff, inadequate supervision on the corridors, in the playground and dining area, poor classroom teaching, unsuitable accommodation and inappropriate curriculum are some of the precursors of behavioural problems in schools. The individual subject teacher may have little if any control over most of these factors and may have to operate as best he can in the given circumstances.

So what can a teacher do to establish a good teaching environment in his classroom? The old adage that 'work prevents trouble', while boredom leads to it, applies. Good classroom management involves having an appropriate amount of material prepared, and a plan of instruction ready for each class. The preparation can be elaborate, and sometimes needs to be. At other times, it may merely amount to corridor preparation: the thinking out of things on the way to class. In all cases, it should involve preparing yourself mentally; calming and steadying yourself so that you remain in control no matter what happens.

Conflict in the classroom does not arise in a vacuum; it develops in a context. A serious breach of discipline is usually preceded by a series of small but significant incidents, in which students test the ground to see what the teacher is like and how much they can get away with. Seemingly innocent requests to go to the toilet, enquiries about the marital status of the teacher and about where they live, or references to the teacher's car are all initial probes by the students to find out if the new teacher is friendly. Is she 'a soft touch', easily diverted into revelatory conversation? Does he know his stuff? Is this teacher 'sussed'? Does he know the school rules? What will she allow to go unchallenged? Is the teacher unsure of his role?

Class discipline can be compared to a circle that can be expanded but not contracted. Many teachers, for the first few weeks of the school year, whilst they are establishing initial control over a new class, are studiously polite but distant, formal, strict, and very diligent in maintaining order, enforcing the school rules, and checking everything. During this period they consistently apply the school discipline system in the case of any student who persistently misbehaves and who, despite being warned, continues to disrupt the class. This student may be probing and testing to see how far he can go with the new teacher. Therefore, for the sake of the class as a whole, and the creation of a learning environment, it may be necessary for the teacher to invoke the full rigour of the school disciplinary system, and show the class that they have teeth! Some teachers find this period of high level strictness difficult to maintain. However, once they have the measure of the new class, and have established a satisfactory degree of control, they can relax the classroom atmosphere to a level that is appropriate for that class group and which they can maintain.

A teacher's approach and demeanour in one class may be very different to that employed in another. Generally speaking, teachers have to be stricter with KS3 than with KS4 and above. Year 7 pupils are energetic and find it more difficult to contain themselves than their older counterparts. They lack the maturity that is required for a more open style of classroom management. Year 12 and 13 students, on the other hand, are adults, or nearly so, and need to be treated accordingly.

Good classroom management entails not only dealing with problems that have arisen, but also with preventing them arising in the first place. For one teacher a group of students may be well behaved and focused on their work, but with another the same class may act as an unruly mob. The following are some ideas which may be helpful to teachers who find themselves in the latter situation.

■ Combating behaviour problems

Tone

Teachers must use 'warm firmness'. Firmness is achieved by use of what Kounin (1977) calls 'high message clarity'. By this he means that the teacher conveys 'I mean it' and 'now' in a desist order. This tone is amplified by the teacher stopping previous activity, giving a warning signal, using a firm tone of voice accompanied by a fixed stare, moving to a different location in the room or approaching the student who is misbehaving. It also involves the follow-through, which entails moving closer to the deviant, looking firmly at him during, and for a while after, the instruction. It is very important to maintain eye contact during this interaction.

The tone of voice is important. A calm, steady voice exudes confidence, and this is amplified by a relaxed demeanour. A shrill tone of voice, on the other hand, coupled with an over-vigilant, tense and aggressive attitude suggests an insecurity on the teacher's part – as if they are actually expecting problems. Students will sense this and start the process of probing and testing, to see how much this teacher can take. Eventually, as the students grow bolder and more confident, the teacher will find it harder and harder to exert any control over the class.

Clarity

High message clarity also means being specific and focused when making statements. 'Ted and Alex, stop talking; now. [pause] Open your books at page 16 and do Question 4 Exercise 7C', is a clear message that does not leave any room for ambiguity or debate. By contrast, 'There is too much noise down the back' is not specific; it is not directed at anyone and is likely to be ignored. Students generally regard vague injunctions as applying to somebody other than themselves.

The role of eye contact

Eye contact plays a very significant role in all interpersonal communications. It can provide information about another's intentions and feelings. It is particularly important in communicating power and preference and, in this respect, teachers should be aware of its role in their interactions with students. In many cases, eye contact will be simultaneously broken or avoided, but often one person will look away first. To avert one's gaze first, particularly with a downward glance, is a submissive signal. Tension will build up as each continues to stare, and the one who looks away has found it necessary to relieve that tension. Eye contact also implies 'presence', the presence of the teacher in the teacher role and their awareness of the power and authority that go with that.

When reprimanding students, many teachers demand that students look directly at them when they are being spoken to. When a student complies, the teacher can be fairly sure that the student is actually listening to what is being said. Teachers are aware that students can easily express insubordination, boredom, or a lack of respect by deliberately looking away, 'throwing her eyes to heaven' or by breaking visual contact in a non-deferential way. Students can be very adept at shutting teachers off by withholding eye contact. At the same time, teachers must bear in mind that a student's inability to look at them may be an indication that this child has difficulty in this regard. Children who have been subjected to violence at home find it particularly difficult to hold eye contact because, in an abusive situation, to do so is to be provocative and may incur the wrath of the abuser. There may also be cultural differences which result in a student being unwilling to give eye contact to an adult. As the professional, a teacher should be aware of and respect such differences.

The control exercised in communication by appropriate eye contact is very subtle, but it is one clear way that teachers can communicate that they are secure and confident in their authority.

Use of territory

Humans, like animals, are sensitive to territorial imperatives. In the conventionally arranged classroom, with the students in rows facing the front, the teacher's area is at the front by the board. If the teacher seldom ventures out among the students, they will develop the notion of the 'teacher's space' (up at the front) and 'our space' (the rest of the classroom). It is important, therefore, for the teacher to move freely, easily and often around the room, alert for signs of incipient trouble. This use of territory by the teacher is another way of conveying status, dominance and confidence in his role.

The way a teacher uses the personal space of a student can also signify differences in status. An indirect approach, looking at a student's work and squatting down to his level, is not threatening, whereas looking directly down at the student from on high can be unsettling. One teacher recalls an occasion when she had warned a troublesome student to stop talking and to get on with his work. The boy was talking yet again and was annoying his neighbours, so the teacher, who was at the back of the room, approached quietly from behind and leant close to his ear, saying quietly, 'Take your books and work at the front'. The boy was half out of his seat before the teacher had finished speaking and had to be reminded to bring his books with him. A sudden invasion of personal space, particularly if unexpected, can help a teacher assert his or her authority particularly in cases where it appears it might be challenged.

While addressing a class, a teacher should move about the room, making brief eye contact with the students, where appropriate. The teacher should treat the personal space and territory of the students with respect, but if necessary enter into those areas in a direct and immediate way, when wishing to convey a dominant attitude. If, for example, the teacher notices a student fiddling with his pen while she is explaining something on the board, she can approach the student and, without interrupting the flow of the lesson, or even looking at him, gently remove the pen from his hand, place it on the desk and continue addressing the class without a pause.

Scanning

An experienced teacher will often see trouble developing at an early stage and defuse it at source. For example, students will always look up to see where the teacher is located in the room before they misbehave. So, while the class is engaged in some assignment, the teacher frequently scans the class to observe what is going on with the students. If a student appears as if she is about to talk to a classmate or to interrupt the work in some way, simply dropping her name 'Jennifer' into the sentence, and, ... pausing ..... (accompanied by a fixed stare) is generally sufficient to let the student know that the teacher is aware of what is going on and that she is to return to task. This can be achieved without interrupting the smooth flow of the lesson.

Smart comments

Smart comments are a common method of probing used by students when trying to ascertain what kind of a person their new teacher is. A student may pass some remark, drop in a swear word, comment on the teacher's appearance, 'slag off' another student in the class, or use a teacher's first name in order to see how the teacher will react and how much they can get away with. All such comments must be challenged, despite the temptation to ignore them. If these minor probes are not confronted, the students will lose respect for the teacher; such comments will become routine and the students will become bolder in their challenges to the teacher's authority.

When a student makes a comment that the teacher finds offensive or insulting, she should stop the class, order the student to stand up and to repeat the comment, move closer to the student and ask, 'What did you say?' If the student refuses to repeat the comment, then the teacher can repeat what she understood the student to say, and explain how she feels about such comments and that she will not tolerate such behaviour in her class. The teacher must not be afraid to repeat verbatim what she overheard. A display of controlled, genuine anger at this stage should be sufficient to discourage others from any further incursions in that domain. The student can remain standing, and when the lesson is over, the teacher can then decide what further action, if any, is necessary.

At times like this, head-on confrontation is appropriate. What is vital for the survival of teachers it that they assert themselves sufficiently to such a degree that the students no longer try it on with them. Later we will consider more sophisticated ways of dealing with such challenges, but they will not make this method obsolete.

Insubordination by demeanour

Often in negative interactions with students, what teachers find objectionable is not what the students actually say but rather their disrespectful tone of voice, the sneering facial expression or the slouched body posture with hands in the pockets. The insubordination is not explicit but implied in their demeanour. As long as this behaviour is hidden and not alluded to, it has power. Such latent undermining of the teacher can be countered by making it visible and explicit. For example: 'Mary, just now you said…, I feel…, I find your tone of voice… (*be as specific as possible in naming what is bothering you*)… highly disrespectful. I object to…' Making visible the non-verbal cue, and the direct declaration of its unacceptability, combined with the teacher confronting the student directly, as one human being to another, can defuse this attempt to undermine the teacher.

Confidence

Confidence is an elusive quality that comes slowly, with experience. When teachers feel confident and self-assured, there is an implication that they expect the students to respond appropriately, and this is usually what happens. When students can sense a teacher's authority they are unlikely to challenge it.

Teachers' confidence is boosted by their ability to define who responds to whom. If, for example, a teacher responds to every question the students put to her, it implies that she lacks confidence and feels uncertain about her ability to gain the students' attention and to dictate the direction of the lesson. By choosing, when necessary, not to respond to students' questions and by making them respond verbally to her, a teacher begins to exercise control over the communication in the classroom.

How do teachers convey confidence, even when they are not feeling confident? The use of body posture: openness of arm position, a sideways lean, tilt of the head, forward lean, close proximity to the addressee and strong eye contact are all elements of a confident demeanour. While a confident person can amplify these, to suggest that it is easy would further undermine those who have difficulty in this respect. As MacGrath (1998) writes, 'Our confidence in teaching is often linked to a belief in our own authority as a teacher, that we do, indeed, have the right to take charge of the class and make things happen in the lesson.' Conscious and sustained work at enhancing one's own self-esteem is often necessary, and for many teachers this may involve a serious investment, in time and energy, on personal development and assertiveness training. (See Appendix 1.)

Dealing with trouble

Despite the fact that the teacher has prepared the lesson in advance, organised the classroom environment and called the class to order, there will inevitably be at least one student in every class who will continue to try and disrupt the lesson. Discretion being the better part of valour, on occasion it may be wise for the teacher to selectively ignore minor incidents in order to avoid interrupting the flow of the lesson. In other cases, subtle hints (pauses, dropping names, or the use of eye contact) may be sufficient. Teachers can minimise the damage that minor troublemakers cause by sitting them alone or at the margins of the class, which amounts to moving them off stage.

If the student does not catch on and take the hint, then it will be necessary to stop the lesson and give one clear formal warning, naming the student(s) involved, stating clearly what behaviour the teacher is objecting to, suggesting a positive alternative, and pointing out the consequences that will follow, if the misbehaviour continues. When all attempts by the teacher to be sympathetic, to appeal to the student's better nature, and to give them a chance fail to change the student's behaviour, it will be obvious that these actions are not seen by the student as kindness, but as weakness and indecisiveness on the teacher's part. Confrontation between the teacher and the student will be unavoidable.

Most people find confrontation unpleasant and try, as far as they can, to avoid it. The responsibility of the teacher, however, is to teach the whole class and not to pander to the tyranny of a few disruptive students. When it comes to the 'crunch', there is a professional requirement of a subject teacher to (a) be able to assess the situation that has arisen, (b) know what to do, and (c) have the courage to do it. One of the demands of teaching is the requirement to make decisions, judge situations accurately, and take appropriate action when dealing with incidents of indiscipline. In Part 3 more sophisticated and subtle methods of handling incidents of indiscipline are considered, but for the moment let us remain in coercive mode and deal with punishments and their administration.

What action a teacher takes in any given situation will depend on how serious he judges the misbehaviour to be.

For minor incidents, *a note in the student's school diary*, to be acknowledged and signed by the parents, may be sufficient. Such a note is most effective when it calls for some response from the parent that will bring the parent and the student together to solve a problem or explore some issue. The tone of the note is important. The content needs to be such that a spirit of cooperation is allowed for, as opposed to a confrontation being provoked. For example: 'Students are expected to arrive in class on time. I have spoken to Paul repeatedly about this but to no avail. I am now at the stage where I feel it necessary to issue a Report Card. Please let me know if you can work something out with Paul that can help us to avoid this.' Clear communication with the parents by means of such notes, in the school diary, by telephone or letters posted home, is an important first step in any discipline code. If no satisfactory resolution is arrived at in this manner, then the issuing of a Report Card will be the natural consequence of the misbehaviour.

If the student persists in misbehaving, or a serious breach of discipline occurs, then the teacher has no alternative but to administer a sanction as a deterrent, appropriate to and following closely on the offence. At this juncture the teacher should say and do as little as possible. The tone of voice is kept polite, short and firm. Avoid getting into excuses or getting involved in 'whys' as these lead to endless argument and confusion. The use of 'I statements' by the teacher is very effective in making the interaction with the student real and immediate. They allow the personality of the teacher to emerge from behind the mask of the teacher role. 'I am very angry because....., I will not accept your.....'

Teachers do some of the following things when trying to cope with incidents of misbehaviour in the classroom:

> *In the case of minor incidents, such as repeated talking or distracting others, a teacher might ask a student to stand by the wall, at the back of the classroom. This isolates the student. It allows the student to cool down from the 'high' of being giddy, and conveys the serious view the teacher is taking of her behaviour. Teachers are careful not to use this sanction too much. They will never have more than one or two students standing at the back at any one time. Overuse of this tactic can devalue its impact.*

For more serious misbehaviour, such as persistent failure to pay attention in class, inability to continue reading from where a previous student stopped reading, or not attempting homework, etc., a teacher might tell a student to copy a number of pages from a textbook, as a punishment. The number of pages must be reasonable and in proportion to the misdemeanour. When giving this punishment, the teacher should insist that it is completed neatly and presented at the beginning of the lesson the following day. Failure to complete the punishment fully would lead to detention. The writing of 'lines' is a pointless and soul destroying exercise.

Serious interruptions to the lesson, such as shouting or jeering, not allowing other students to participate in class, etc., may require ordering the student to leave the classroom altogether. Most schools have arrangements made to allow for this. Students sent out of class may have to spend time with the head of department, year head or another colleague. Many schools have a room, variously named as the 'withdrawal', 'isolation' or 'inclusion' room, etc., where students go in order to complete work from the lesson out of which they have been sent.

Very serious breaches of discipline, such as throwing things during class, answering back and challenging the teacher, will require that the student is faced with the seriousness of his behaviour. This may involve a period of detention (see below). The teacher may need to fill out details of a serious incident and other members of staff, for example, the tutor or year head may get involved.

It is up to teachers to devise practices that they feel are appropriate in their particular circumstances and that they feel comfortable using.

▓ Detention

Detention is commonly used for serious breaches of discipline. When students are detained they have usually caused considerable disruption and have been warned many times beforehand. Earlier attempts to reason with them have failed to bring about a satisfactory resolution. At this stage the teacher ought not to make any exceptions for games, dental appointments, or part-time jobs. Advance notice is always required for detentions after school to allow parents to make alternative transport arrangements on the day, if necessary. It is inconvenient for the teacher to have to stay in school after classes. However, it may be well worth the investment in time and effort. When students see that the teacher is determined to follow through on cases of indiscipline in class, then the frequency of such incidents will diminish considerably.

Some schools, particularly in rural areas, have detention at lunchtime as this is less problematic in terms of school transport arrangements. Lunchtime detention can be useful in helping teachers deal with minor cases of student misbehaviour. Detention after school however, by virtue of its awkwardness, is more effective. It focuses the attention of the student (and his parents) on the seriousness of his misbehaviour in school.

▓ School Code of Discipline

Every school has (or should have) a graded procedure for dealing with incidents of indiscipline as they arise. Under this Code, a series of minor misdemeanours can lead to the school issuing the student with a Report Card. Sometimes, the initial misbehaviour is of such a serious nature that the teacher feels it necessary to issue a Report Card immediately. This usually means that the matter is reported to the year head or the deputy head, and the student's parents are invited to visit the school and are informed in person about what has taken place. The student is generally put 'On Report' and monitored closely, on a class by class basis, for perhaps a week or more, depending on the seriousness of the misdemeanour.

■ **Exclusion**

With persistent troublemakers, it may be necessary to order the student to leave the classroom for a period of time, to allow for the establishment of a very definite routine and set of expectations of student behaviour in the class. The cooperation of the year head, head or colleagues may be required to effect this. Many schools have a Learning Support Unit, or equivalent, that such students can attend. In addition to giving everyone a break from each other, this offers the student the opportunity of learning in a small group for a while. Ideally, there will also be the chance to explore the difficulties he experiences in the class, as well as any unidentified learning needs, and it is hoped the student may acquire some skills to help him reintegrate.

When a class routine has been established, it will then be possible to reintroduce the troublemaker to the class, after a detailed discussion has taken place and an agreement on behaviour has been arrived at between the student and teacher, witnessed, if necessary, by the year head and parents.

In very serious cases, it may be necessary, after due process, to exclude a student from school for a fixed term.

Sometimes teachers may be so frustrated by the behaviour of a student(s) that they are impatient with the process outlined above, and prefer to unilaterally punish the offender(s). While this may help the teacher to feel powerful and in control, such hasty action can generate some very negative emotions in students, with attendant behaviours. Students who perceive themselves to be victims of what they consider rash punishment are invariably resentful. They may harbour revenge fantasies and seek to get even with the teacher by being passively aggressive (late for class, unenthusiastic, uncooperative) or through more overt activities like vandalism and graffiti. Some such students rebel and persist in doing the opposite to what they are supposed to do, just to prove that they are not beaten. Others become underhand or come to see themselves as bad.

The sad thing is that there is no need for any of this if teachers respect students and are fair in their dealings with them. Whatever sanction is invoked, students must have a sense that it is reasonable and that they could have avoided it, had they acted otherwise. It is sufficient, for example, that a student be required to clean the graffiti off her own table, but there is no need to subject her to a haranguing while she is doing so. Being forced by a teacher to clean all the tables in the room would destroy that student's sense of fair play and the possibility of a positive outcome is diminished. When students are treated respectfully, they are far more likely to act responsibly, and the damage to their self-esteem, the student–teacher relationship, and the class atmosphere is minimised.

Some teachers prefer to deal with incidents of indiscipline on the spot during the lesson, as this has the advantage of immediacy. However, if a teacher is unsure of what to do or senses that she is going to be challenged, then it may be wiser to defer, and order the student(s) involved to remain behind after class to discuss the matter. This ensures that the lesson is not interrupted, and it gives the teacher time to reflect on what to do next. It reduces the possibility of the teacher being drawn into a damaging confrontation in front of the class, and it prevents the student playing to the gallery or the teacher feeling under pressure to win at all costs.

■ Triangulation

If a teacher finds himself at loggerheads with a particular student, it may be necessary to postpone making a decision and to seek the advice and support of colleagues, the tutor, the year head, the SENCO or the deputy head. It is often helpful at this stage to seek an appointment with the student's parents, to inform them of their child's behaviour and to involve them in seeking a solution to the problem. Once a parent, the tutor, year head or a member of the senior management team is involved, the interpersonal dynamic of the conflict alters significantly. This 'triangulation' of the problem removes the boundaries surrounding the conflict and opens it up to the objective scrutiny and the influence of third parties.

■ Meeting the parents

When meeting parents the teacher needs to be sensitive to their situation. Schools can be intimidating places for adults who are not familiar with them, or who have their own painful memories of schools and teachers. To be called to the school to discuss the behaviour of your child is an embarrassing, uncomfortable experience for any parent.

It is helpful to begin the meeting by assuring the parent of your support and of feeding in as much 'positive' about the student as possible, before coming to the behaviour that is objectionable. Parents need support. Sometimes they need ideas on how to be with their children. They need strategies that will give them hope and help them to stay connected with their children when the going gets tough. Parents need to be helped to strengthen their relationship with their children, because it is the strength of this relationship that is the basis of any influence they have. When meeting parents it is best to talk to them alone first. Allow them the space and time to discuss their child and how things are at home. Assure them of your support and request their cooperation in dealing with the present difficulty. Following this discussion, it is a good strategy if both the teacher and the parent can devise a mutually satisfactory plan to help the student to change his behaviour in class. When the student is called into the meeting she or he should receive a brief summary of what has been discussed, and should be made aware of the solidarity and common purpose that exists between the teacher and the parent. Finally, a commitment to abide by the agreed plan should be sought from the student.

This approach is very different to calling in the parents and focusing exclusively on their child's bad behaviour and, by implication, on their own inadequate parenting.

■ Recording

Whatever action teachers decide to take, it is important that they note all serious incidents in the student's diary. Parents often complain that nobody at the school told them what was going on. The note in the student's diary can be a brief description of what happened, the date, and what the teacher did about it. For example, 'Nov 5th: Marie was making unkind comments about other students during French class. When asked to stop she refused and continued to disrupt the class. I have reported the matter to the year head.' Another example might be: 'Feb 8th: Despite being asked to stop, John continued to disrupt the class and talk out of turn. Please talk with John and try to help him see why this behaviour is a problem.' Be as specific and as factual as you can. Report the incident as a video camera would record it. Ask that the parent acknowledge the note by signing it.

Many teachers feel that it is a good idea to note everything in their own class file. They keep an account of transgressions, including the date, details of the incident, who was involved, what ensued, and what action was taken. When written work as punishment is set, they note what was given, to whom, and when it has to be handed in.

It is not helpful to give a blanket punishment to a whole class. It is unfair to the innocent and is guaranteed to make enemies for the teacher. It is much fairer and more effective to target the key troublemakers.

Teachers must be fair and be seen to be fair. They must be consistent and avoid favouritism. This can be difficult because there are always students to whom a teacher is naturally drawn and of whom they think highly. However, the teacher must maintain a high degree of professional objectivity and treat all students fairly and with respect.

■ Emotional clarity

It is important that teachers are aware of what is going on for themselves, emotionally, when in conflict with troublesome students. A teacher's own emotional state can often have a considerable impact on how he is going to handle a situation. For example, if the teacher is feeling hurt, it is likely that he will react by being angry. To teach well, it may be that he needs to learn to deal with his own anger. There are many self-development and personal growth courses available to teachers throughout the country. These have a valuable contribution to make in helping teachers to become more aware of the interpersonal dynamics of the classroom situation and to gain meaningful insight into their own response patterns.

■ Coercive classroom management style

The first two Parts of this book have been written with the needs of teachers at the beginning of their careers specifically in mind. The approach to classroom management described thus far has been coercive, i.e. a stimulus/response approach in which compliance with the wishes of the teacher is achieved by the use or threatened use of punitive action. The teacher assumes complete responsibility for every interaction in the classroom. The teacher may feel the need to maintain order in the classroom by compulsion. The need for this is sometimes based on the teacher's own fear of losing control of the situation and of the class becoming chaotic. Often this is a very real concern.

This method of classroom management is primarily concerned with control and with the completion of the task involved. When put fully into operation it reduces the possibility of any cooperative relationship developing between the students and their teacher. The self-esteem of all parties is threatened and the classroom atmosphere becomes tense and anxious. Often the rules become more important than the children, and the purpose and spirit that inspired them are lost. Motivation is generated by the threat of punishment.

While this approach to classroom management is useful and at times essential in providing short-term control, it is not recommended that a teacher remain in this mode any longer than is necessary. Unfortunately, many teachers fail to move beyond this methodology and continue for all of their teaching careers using coercive approaches to classroom management. At a personal level, the consequences of maintaining this approach and the outlook that accompanies it are considerable. Teachers tend to become brittle, negative and bitter. In the long term, as they approach middle age, they may no longer have the strength or energy to teach in this way and frequently suffer from long-term physical or mental exhaustion.

As teachers gain experience and their confidence as a competent practitioner grows, they can become more flexible and creative in their approach to classroom management. There are other, enabling methods of dealing with children that have been developed by many teachers. These are explored in Part 3.

Preface to Part 3

First day at school

Ireland 1958

Picture a small three-teacher school with about ninety children on the roll. The unvarnished wooden floorboards are caked with mud from the playground and dust glistens in the watery sunlight that streams through the windows set high up in the walls. The windows are supposed to open when a cord is pulled by swivelling along a curved bar with cogs. The cogs are stuck with rust and the cord is knotted. The windows are seldom opened and the ceiling is high so that the rooms can become stuffy while remaining cold. The walls are sheeted with wooden panelling to a height of about three feet. Everything is painted green and smells of dampness.

There is an open fire with a flat stone slab at either side. On cold winter mornings the pupils place lemonade bottles, filled with milk and sealed with paper corks, on the slabs to warm. From time to time a bottle cracks so that the smell of burnt milk drifts upwards in the stale air to join the resident smells of chalk dust, sweat, urine and fear. Around the fire is a railing with upright bars set about three inches apart. It protrudes about fifteen inches into the crowded classroom and obstructs the passage way to the front of the teacher's table. On cold winter mornings the children are sometimes permitted to warm their frozen hands at the fire, which is never really enthusiastic about coming to life. The railing is big and heavy. The children are shy, withdrawn, unkempt, full of irrepressible energy, cheeky, lazy and according to the master they are all 'clearly in need of being taught manners'.

There is no running water in the school, not even a tap in the yard. The toilets are outside. After a child has 'done the necessary', it is expected to take a shovel and cover its 'shame' with ashes from the school fire.

The benches seat six children and have a sloping top. There is a recess for the inkwell and an indentation to stop pens rolling to the floor. They invariably do. Nibs are bent and broken. Ink is spilt. Copies are daubed. Inkwells are fiddled with. The children are beaten routinely.

The teacher has an ash stick, eighteen inches long and about the thickness of a man's middle finger. The bark has been peeled off. It is white in colour with the ends pared round. Beating usually takes the form of slaps on the open palm of the hand and ranges from one slap on each hand to 'six of the best'. The severity varies from the ineffectual taps of the Mistress to the practiced cuts of the Master. Through the use of this stick obedience is instilled, laziness is rooted out and downright evil and sin eradicated. Beating on the bottom involves an additional shaming and is reserved for children who have no parents to come to the school and threaten the Master.

Pat Murphy was a five-year-old boy who was being fostered by an elderly couple on a remote farm about two miles from the school. He was a 'problem child', obviously disturbed but by no means stupid. His first day at school was mine also. He was beaten on the backside with the stick on our first day for some minor misdemeanour which I cannot recall. I do, however, have a vivid recollection of a subsequent occasion not long afterwards when the mistress tried to administer a slap on the backside to Pat and in the process he bit her hand. Clearly a 'devilish act'.

After lunch Pat was dragged from room to room by the Master and beaten savagely on the bottom in front of every child in the school as a punishment for his 'evil misdeed' and as a means of ensuring that his evil ways would not spread throughout the school. Two sixth class boys were called upon to assist the Master. They prised Pat's fingers from desks, the bars on the fireguard, or from the corners of the green woodwork as he screamed for mercy and tried to cling on in panic to whatever was nearby. His cries of 'I won't do it anymore' filled every molecule of space in the room both inside and outside my head. Pat's screaming was interpreted by the Master as further testimony of a degraded character as punishment was supposed to be suffered in silence. Clearly this 'bucko' had a lot to learn! My class occupied an end room and Pat was beaten before us twice that day.

How it ended I do not know. What was said I do not remember. I was four years old. I was enraged. I was terrified. I stayed quiet. So did the other teachers. So did all the parents who heard about it. So did my father the local Garda Sergeant. So did the whole community. There was a belief that Pat, an illegitimate child, probably deserved the beating. The Master was after all a pillar of society, a fervent Catholic, a fanatical gaelgoir, a vocal supporter of the GAA, and a prominent member of Fianna Fail who was later appointed to the Senate.

I was traumatised on that day. The fear and anger that consumed me have been with me for over forty years. My experiences a few years later at the Christian Brothers only added to my sense of horror and outrage. The violence was never again as explosive as in that early experience, but its routine, systematic use by many of the brothers and by many of the lay teachers, combined with the intensity of those who used it, made it even worse.

I have no wish to sully the good name of anyone alluded to here. It is my earnest wish that they remain anonymous and in peace. The story itself is not unique. These teachers were both a product and an agent of the culture, of their time. They were good men doing what they thought was right.

When I became a teacher in 1972 corporal punishment was still the institutionalised way in Irish schools. As a teacher I was expected to use it but I could not handle that role or even witness it without being really upset. Within two years I had volunteered to become a remedial teacher in an attempt to escape my own pain and to save children like Pat Murphy from the suffering. I developed a way to coexist with disturbed and disadvantaged children without resorting to 'slapping them'. The abolition of corporal punishment in 1984 came as a blessed relief.

In my work as a teacher I have witnessed the ordinary humanity of many teachers shine through despite everything. They have shown me that humour and kindness can be a part of teaching regardless of the circumstances. I never fail to be inspired by the level of commitment to children that is part of the ethic of the majority of those with whom I have worked. My life's work has been a search for a better way to teach.

Harry

Part 3

Enabling approaches to classroom management

They won't always remember what you taught them, but they will never forget how you treated them.

Anon

Children nowadays want more. They want, among other things, more meaningful relationships with adults, and are no longer willing to 'put up and shut up' as they might have in the past, when students were so determined to get on in life that they accepted and tolerated abuse at the hands of their teachers. Many of the old coercive ways of classroom management are no longer acceptable and, therefore, more enabling approaches need to be used in the teaching of the present generation of teenagers.

These approaches, while recognising the need for the containment of student misbehaviour, seek to do this by challenging students to take their share of the responsibility for the conduct of the class and the interactions that take place during lessons. The teacher consciously works on establishing a healthy relationship with the students, so that all involved can experience satisfaction in their work, as opposed to frustration and disillusionment. The relationship thus established strengthens over time and influences the class climate – the context within which teaching, learning and all behaviour takes place. Just as a gardener prepares the ground before any cultivation occurs, the teacher must cultivate a good class atmosphere in order to create the conditions conducive to learning. Students have a need for recognition, to have a say in what is going on, to be involved, to have a laugh and to experience success and achievement at some level. The focus, therefore, is on meeting student needs and on recognising that student misbehaviour is often a misdirected attempt on their part to satisfy these needs.

■ The role of self-esteem in classroom management

Self-esteem has to do with how you feel about your lovability and your capability. It is, according to Humphreys (1995), a term used to describe your own judgement of your worth and importance. It is formed by the messages received and taken in, about oneself, from significant others. Dorothy Corkille Briggs sums it up as follows:

> *A person's judgment of self influences the kind of friends he chooses, how he gets along with others, the kind of person he marries and how productive he will be. It affects his creativity, integrity, stability and even whether he will be a leader or a follower. His feeling of self worth forms the core of his personality and determines the use he makes of his aptitudes and abilities. His attitude towards himself has a direct bearing on how he lives all parts of his life. In fact, self-esteem is the mainspring that slates each of us for success or failure as a human being.*

The concept of self-esteem does not, of itself, provide a full explanation of how students and teachers react to each other as they do. Knowledge of the concept can, however, provide valuable insights into our understanding of the underlying causes behind the different behaviours students adopt when they interact with teachers.

Everything a teacher does or says is evaluated by students, in terms of its impact on their status and self-esteem. Often during an altercation between a teacher and a student, much of what is classified as 'cheeky' or insolent, by the teacher, is an attempt by the student, albeit a misguided one, to preserve their esteem or status in front of their peers. At the same time, the teacher is also attempting to do the same. Not surprisingly, when insecure teachers, who feel that they must be in total control and win at all costs, are confronted by disaffected students with nothing to lose, a seemingly minor incident can very quickly escalate into a serious confrontation.

A great number of students enjoy school. They come with sufficient self-esteem and belief in themselves to be able to mix reasonably well with their classmates and to cope with whatever success, disappointment, rejection, failure, or frustration everyday life throws at them. They worry about being accepted by their friends but are not excessively dependent on them. By and large, they are successful in school and get on well with most of the teachers. They are self-motivated because they know what they want and where they are going in terms of a career. There is a high degree of congruity and agreement between the parents of these students and the school system. The parents are involved with, and are supportive of, their children. They take every opportunity to encourage, praise and acknowledge their achievements and efforts.

The school system values and accepts these students. The teachers communicate openly and directly with them, display a high degree of flexibility, where necessary, in applying the school rules, reinforce and praise their achievements and generally trust the students to behave responsibly. These students in turn find it easy to be close to authority figures and are able to work things out with them. The interactions between students and teachers are multifaceted and comprehensive. The students validate the system and teachers proudly point to them as examples of how students should behave. For a great many people, the system works.

However, there are many other students whose experiences in school are not need-satisfying. Relationships with teachers are fraught with conflict. Learning is associated with frustration and failure. Many of these children, from their first day at school, come with a low sense of self-worth. These students are extremely concerned about what other people think, are in constant need of reassurance, lack autonomy and individuality, and are extremely fearful of making mistakes. They expend a great deal of energy boasting, wanting to impress others, showing off or trying to prove that they are right. They frequently display a negative attitude to everything, and it appears that they can't be pleased. They feel everything is unfair, think that others are always better off, habitually find fault, blame others and generally have a 'chip on their shoulder'. Their opinions and outlook are rigid and inflexible, and they habitually make fun of and slag off others. They are fearful and derisive of anything different to what they consider to be the norm. All these behaviours and attitudes are manifestations of low self-esteem and for these students life is difficult.

Low self-esteem comes from such growing up experiences as absence of affection and lack of encouragement, as a child. In order to develop high self-esteem children need affection and encouragement. The love they receive needs to be given as a gift, not conditional on performance or compliance. Children need to feel secure in their relationship with parents, who are sensitive to their fear of rejection. They need lots of praise, recognition and respect. If the home atmosphere is permeated by fear, violence, criticism, ridicule, sarcasm and cynicism, the conditions listed above cannot be fulfilled. Children from such homes tend to have low self-esteem.

One noteworthy characteristic of people with low self-esteem is their extreme concern about what others think. The first 'others' are parents, but there may also be 'significant others' like grandparents, child-minders, or older brothers and sisters who are involved in the parenting. The child's experience in the home environment creates a kind of 'blueprint' for future relationships. In primary school, early years and KS1 teachers become important 'significant others'. How accepting they are of children, how sensitive they are to their world and how they relate to children is very important.

By the time students get to secondary school, low achievers have probably given up trying to impress their teachers. Generally speaking, during the teenage years the 'significant others' for the low achiever are his classmates. He can impress them by being the most cheeky or defiant student in the class, by being constantly late, the most independent 'hard man', the best laugh or by being as objectionable as possible to teachers. When disruptive students draw a teacher into conflict, their status is raised within their peer group. It is helpful, therefore, when a teacher is dealing with such students, to do so on a one-to-one basis, after class, when the student is free from the support or the pressure of his peer audience. During the lesson, teachers should keep their exchanges with these students brief, and create as little fuss as possible in dealing with whatever situation arises. Low achieving students with low self-esteem are very needy and will use any opportunity to disrupt the class, get it off task, and distract attention from their own inadequacies.

In all interactions with such students the teacher should be mindful that what they need most in life is esteem boosting, as opposed to being put down. The instinct in the education system and of teachers generally, acting out of concern for themselves, is to put these troublemakers in their place, by subjecting them to punishment, detention or exclusion. However, this approach simply does not work in the long term. Despite all the detentions, punishment and verbal haranguing, the same names keep coming up again and again on the lists of students who cause trouble.

We have found through our years of teaching disadvantaged children, that boosting the esteem of chronic troublemakers is an effective way of bringing about positive changes in their behaviour. By working systematically on enhancing students' self-esteem, both as individuals and as class groups, teachers can begin to dissolve many of the problems that sap their energy. The students in turn begin to see their teachers as real persons and come to value the relationship that develops between the teachers and themselves. The amount of real influence a teacher has is a function of that relationship.

The last thing that teachers should do is to continue the cycle of neglect or abuse that gave rise to low self-esteem in the first place. This is, unfortunately, what schools often do when faced with the challenge of dealing with students from dysfunctional families, who are in difficulty. The school system itself can be very destructive of esteem when there is an insistence on rigid conformity, supported by a 'policing style' of supervision, and a judicial punishment routine. Practices within the school administration system such as streaming can often add to a student's feeling of worthlessness. This is further compounded by the negative attitude of some teachers towards students who are 'different' or 'weak'.

While the individual teacher may be able to do very little about the managerial practices of the school, there are practical things that a teacher can do to help raise the self-esteem of students regardless of the subject being taught.

> *Healthy people see themselves as liked, wanted, acceptable, able and worthy. Not only do they feel that they are people of dignity and worth, but they behave as though they were. Indeed, it is in this factor of how a person sees himself, that we are likely to find the most outstanding differences between high and low self-image people. It is not the people who feel that they are liked and wanted and acceptable and able who fill our prisons and mental hospitals. Rather, it is those who feel deeply inadequate, unliked, unwanted, unacceptable and unable.*

> Hamachek

Things teachers can do to raise the self-esteem of students

How you are with them

Your own attitude towards young people is a crucial element in how you relate as a teacher to a class of adolescents. It permeates and colours all your interactions with them. It is immediately obvious to students whether you like them or not. It helps if you can stop seeing yourself as a 'maths teacher' or an 'English teacher' but rather as a *teacher* who happens to be teaching maths or English to a group of students at a given time.

'I'm right!'

Everybody wants to get it right. To avoid the sense of failure only give work to the students that they are capable of doing. Lessen the impact on 'no-hopers' by asking them questions to which they know the answer. Ask weak students easy questions. Involve everybody in the process of the lesson, not just the more able. If a student has answered a question incorrectly, return to him soon afterwards with an easier question thereby giving him a chance to be right. Everyone wants to be right.

Boost morale

One thing you might try is to preface questions to low self-esteem students with a positive comment. You might say, 'This is a hard question, Tom, and you're a man who knows what's going on so what do you think of.....', or 'Bill, you are our expert on unusual facts, what is the meaning of the term.....' By prefacing the question with remarks like these, the teacher buoys students up, so that they feel good about themselves and will not be too hurt if they get the wrong answer.

'Well done'

Set work so there is always something to praise! 'Denis, you laid out this work very neatly and the beginning is really good.' Even if the teacher has to subsequently correct the rest of the work, the compliment will encourage the students to take pride in their work. They need to believe that they 'can do' the task set, that they are good enough, before they will commit themselves to trying. Did you know that there are 42 ways to say well done (see page 79)?

Weak students with low self-esteem are hypersensitive to criticism of any sort, so the tone a teacher adopts is crucial. When correcting students' work (or behaviour) it is helpful if the teacher can see the positive in the students. Look for what is right first and keep criticism to a minimum. 'Well done, Sarah. You did the last exercise very well and you got the first part of this answer correct. Now look at this bit. What you have to remember is.....', or 'Paul, I know that you are excited and I understand why, but it's not OK to shout out in my class like that'.

Learn from mistakes

Mistakes are positive and are an integral part of learning any skill. Teachers can do a lot to create a climate in their classes where it is acceptable to make mistakes. Praise a student if he answers a question incorrectly, because it shows that he is making an effort and that he is trying. Mistakes are an opportunity for learning. 'I'm glad you made that mistake, Lucy, because it is a very common error and you reminded me to point out that.....' Teachers need to be vigilant and quick to intervene if there is any sign of making fun of a student by classmates when he makes a mistake.

'It's useless'

Sometimes, when a student is in despair and is frustrated, they can be difficult to help. No matter what the teacher tries to do, it is no good. The use of the phrase, 'How can I help you get this right?' is often useful in this situation because it puts the onus on the student to define the problem instead of criticising every effort the teacher is making.

Non-verbal communication

A discreet non-verbal signal is often preferable to a public verbal reprimand. Students with low self-esteem often feel that they must answer back when they feel put down. Non-verbal communication can get students back on task with the minimum of fuss. A wink, a nod, or some other gesture can be just as effective, and is less challenging, than a verbal exchange. When a teacher, for example, finds that some students are not paying attention, instead of pouncing on them in an attempt to catch them out, it is better to get the students back on track, quietly, using non-verbal cues.

Accept poor concentration

Many students find it very difficult to stay on task for any length of time. Be gentle. Like a good shepherd, the teacher, from time to time in the lesson, may need to gently, but firmly, call back his straying flock.

Acceptance of students' culture

A good way of keeping lines of communication open with students is to be aware of, and ask about their TV viewing, their music, their fashion and sport. Students love to be asked about their culture and terminology. 'What is lipsin or a bare breeze? How would a chav dress?' It is not necessary for a teacher to know the answers to such questions. A vague interest on the part of the teacher is sufficient. Students will be more than happy to 'teach the teacher', if the teacher is open to learning. Students love any opportunity to demonstrate their knowledge and expertise in an area of life about which the teacher is ignorant. This kind of role reversal helps to build positive relationships between teachers and their students. Teachers who 'tune in' to students and who are 'on the ball' have power, because they are more likely to have a relationship with the students that is based on reality.

If teachers enter teenage culture in a positive way, respecting their ideas, and looking for what is of value in the things that they enjoy, then they will be given opportunities to help their students to learn and to grow in awareness. Teachers can discuss with their students'

issues such as, labels/brand names on fashion clothes, the high cost of trainers, underage drinking, or part-time working. Whilst taking care to observe boundaries and maintain their distance, teachers can do much to increase their 'with-it-ness quotient' and foster a healthy relationship with their students.

Learn about the students

It helps to strengthen the teachers' relationship with students if they know as much as possible (without being intrusive) about the students' families, their pastimes, pets, hobbies, and their out-of-school achievements. This enquiry and exchange of knowledge allow the students to teach the teacher, and enables the teacher to make contact with the students as real people. These interests can also provide material to illustrate points in subsequent lessons.

Observe social niceties

'Good morning', 'Have a nice weekend'. Ask about students who are sick, bereaved or in hospital. 'Did anybody visit Jim in hospital? How is Peter's mum after her operation?'

42 ways of saying well done

I like that   That's terrific   Good work   Excellent

That's better   You're doing fine   One more try and you have it

Keep up the good work   Exactly right   That's a good idea

Good for you   Nice one   Now that's what I call a fine job

That's the best you have ever done   I knew you could do it

You're doing that much better today   That's RIGHT

That's coming along nicely   Keep working at it, it's improving

Great stuff   That's much better   Fantastic

You really worked hard today   Great   That's it

You're really learning a lot   That's the way to do it

You're doing nicely   That's good   Congratulations

That's better than ever   Wow, that IS good   Wonderful

Fine   I do like that   Good stuff   Brilliant

You're really improving all the time   A1   Well done

Well, look at you now   You must have been practising

Teaching a 'difficult' class

I've come to the frightening conclusion that I am the decisive element in the classroom.
It is my personal approach that creates the climate.
It's my daily mood that makes the weather.
As a teacher, I possess tremendous power to make a child's life miserable or joyous,
I can be a tool of torture or an instrument of inspiration.
I can humiliate or humour, hurt or heal.
In all situations, it is my response that decides whether a crisis will be escalated or de-escalated, and a child humanised or dehumanised.
I do make a difference.

Chaim Ginott

Teaching can vary from being a very satisfying experience in one class, to being a struggle to survive in another. With one group the teacher gets work done, the students learn, results tend to be good and there is a sense of achievement, both for the teacher and the students. The students in these classes are well motivated, show respect for their teachers, value their judgements and endeavour to get everything they can from the school experience. The teacher in turn is energised by contact with these classes.

In schools that practice rigid streaming, there are, however, other classes about whom teachers will say things like, 'No matter what I do with them, I don't seem to be able to get through to them. They are impossible. I've tried everything with them. I'm exhausted from them. I can't wait for the holidays.' The requirement that teachers prepare such classes for examinations is bordering on the impossible. Often the students in these classes are simply not able to take academic subjects to examination level. While some students fail, many pass only because of the experience and cunning of the teacher in choosing the topics that come up in the exam papers or in preparing 'catch all' answers. In the 'wide ability' or high schools in areas that retain the Eleven Plus exam, these classes are, of course, more common.

Such 'difficult' classes drain teachers of energy because to maintain even a semblance of order demands that the teacher must be in a state of constant alert. In such a classroom, progress is tortuously slow. More time is spent correcting students than in teaching them. The rules are constantly being tested. Students sit anywhere except where they are supposed to. There is constant interruption and hassle. Books are lost or torn. Writing equipment is missing or broken. Pens 'run out'. Materials are forgotten. The obstacles to progress are endless. If the teachers drop their guard even for a moment, a scene can develop quickly, and if it is not checked, it will get out of hand, leading to the possibility that someone will get hurt or property will be damaged. The teachers' work on behalf of the students is unappreciated and they experience a sense of powerlessness and frustration. Even the most committed teachers begin to lose energy and confidence when exposed to the relentless negativity in these classes. While experienced teachers organise things so that opportunities to cause disruption are minimised, class contact remains draining and unsatisfactory.

What are the elements that so radically alter the dynamics in one class as opposed to the other? While there are many factors involved, the most critical ones are the social, cultural and family background, from which each group of students come. In the case of the 'good' class, there is often a high degree of compatibility between the values, behavioural norms, and aspirations of the parents of these students and those of their teachers. The parents know the 'score', as far as school is involved. They probably have a good relationship with their children and can help them in their involvement with their teachers. The students have a history of positive experiences with authority figures, as exemplified by their parents, and this in turn feeds positively into the student–teacher relationship.

The key word here is relationship. When a teacher enters the classroom of the 'good' class, he is walking into a situation where the existence of a positive relationship is taken for granted. The stronger the relationship or bond between the students and the teacher, the greater will be the influence of that teacher in the classroom.

In the case of the 'difficult' class, the converse is likely to be the case. Very often there is a low degree of correspondence between the culture, behavioural norms, expectations and ambitions of the students and those of the teachers and the school. In dealing with the students, without even being aware of it, teachers can be patronising in their concern and often cloak their fear and hostility in self-righteousness and rules. The students do not experience their involvement with the teachers or the school as 'need-satisfying'. Indeed, they often detach themselves completely and insulate themselves from the pain of failure and the emotionally chilling effect of teachers' disapproval. When this happens, the students give up altogether and move outside the sphere of influence of their teachers. They remain in school only on sufferance, and any messing about or trouble is a welcome relief from the pain of failure and the boredom induced by captivity. These students are likely to be in constant conflict with their parents, who sometimes have given up on their children. In this situation, teachers have to work very hard at building positive relationships with these students and while this is difficult, it is by no means impossible.

The relationship between the individual teacher and the students in a class is, in our view, the most important element in the teacher's classroom management strategy. It is more a matter of how the teacher is with the students, rather than what is done with them. How teachers approach the students, talk to them, the tone they use, how they relate and react to them are the crucial elements in creating the class atmosphere, conducive to either warm cooperation or varying degrees of disruption, rebellion and hostility.

A teacher can teach a 'good' class without having to work consciously at forming a relationship with the students. The shared work in hand, coupled with the students' ability and ambition, is sufficient to ensure that both teacher and class have a sense of common purpose. All parties are highly motivated and committed to the task in hand.

With a 'difficult' class, however, the establishment of a bond between the teacher and the students is a prerequisite to any learning taking place. The creation, by the teacher, of a positive class atmosphere is a key factor that can facilitate students' learning and reduce the incidence of conflict in the class. It is only when teachers have established good relationships between themselves and their students, that they can turn their attention fully to the actual teaching activity.

It is also interesting to note the role of expectation in relation to this. In a sense, there is often a cycle linking our expectations with the kind of relationships we tend to develop. As MacGrath (1998) writes, 'How we expect someone to behave often influences how we perceive and interpret his or her behaviour and there is evidence to suggest that a positive attitude towards pupils is associated with fewer difficulties with discipline, (for example, see Hargreaves, Hestor and Mellor 1975).' The very act of perceiving a class as a 'good' one can, therefore, contribute to its 'good' behaviour. The opposite is, of course, unfortunately also true.

Consider the qualities of any good relationship, be it between members of a family, friends or partners. What do we observe? They do things together. They have shared goals. There is a feeling of community, of belonging between the parties. There is the possibility of a bit of fun in the interactions. Respect is part of the dynamic of the relationship. Politeness and consideration permeate all interactions and the atmosphere is generally positive. In this kind of relationship, people learn from and have influence on each other. When we think about the things that foster and nourish such a relationship, we can begin to apply that knowledge to relationships in the classroom, where similar outcomes are sought.

Some teachers seem to have a natural ability to create a positive learning environment in their classrooms and to be able to maintain the respect of their students. How do these teachers establish such a relationship with a class of troublesome adolescents? When asked to reflect on how they approach such classes, these teachers invariably point to some of the following ideas.

■ Some suggestions when teaching a 'difficult' class

Build in success

Nothing succeeds like success. Some students need to experience success quickly, because very often those in difficulty are inclined to give up, even before they start. They need help in coming to believe that they 'can do it' and that for them 40% is excellent. It is a good idea to start with 'low fences'; easy assignments that are guaranteed to give weak students a taste of success. These teachers are not afraid, if necessary, to go right back to basics, in order to find something that these students are able to do successfully. Once the students are on a roll of success, the teacher can gradually introduce them to more difficult material and slowly bring them up to the standard required. Failure to begin with what they know only leads to frustration in the end.

No one likes to look foolish. Students have a need to be seen as important among their peers. They do not want to lose face and will often aggressively do nothing, rather than attempt some task with the risk that they might fail. To overcome this fear of failure they need constant encouragement to take a chance and try. Comments such as 'You're well able for this. Now! see you can do it. You're better than you think. Look at that! Well done. That bit is very good' (even if the rest is incorrect), are encouraging and help students to re-evaluate their negative assessment of themselves, their teachers and school in general.

Coach

Teachers who are successful with 'difficult' classes are generally positively disposed towards their students. They act like a defence lawyer, someone who is on the side of students, and who sees them as young people with something to learn, and not as a bunch of hooligans to be feared and put down. Students need to feel that their teachers are trustworthy, fair and on their side. They can sense if a teacher is someone who is personally interested in their success and is willing to see the good in them. They are perceptive in deciphering the body language of teachers, to ascertain if they like them or not. The more difficult students seem to be particularly astute in this regard.

A similar dynamic can be seen in action when a good coach works with a team. The players know and accept that the coach is going to ask a lot of them but when the relationship is right the team develops a spirit and a sense of self-belief that enables them to perform to their maximum potential. Jimmy Barry Murphy managed the victorious Cork All Ireland hurling team in 1999. Tom Humphries, writing in the *Irish Times*, said of him:

> *You can see it on a drizzly night in Pairc Ui Chaoimh, the young county hurling team he has built and boosted flock around him faithfully. From the outside his approach is no guru, no method; they perform for him because he's the type of guy people want to perform for and quietly he gets his type of hurling out of them with them scarcely being aware of the design.*

A teacher and a coach are alike in the sense that both must watch the field of play, understand emerging configurations, recognise productive possibilities, adapt the pace and have flexible purposing. Fluid intelligence is the hallmark of effectiveness in both arenas. A good teacher communicates like a team coach by encouraging, advising and empowering members of the team, fostering their self-esteem and positively affirming their efforts.

Involvement

Some teachers plan a chart of the course with their students. They explain to their classes how much they would like to have done by Christmas or by the summer. They involve the students in this planning and inform them of their expectations and goals. Students like to know where they are going and they like to be able to check out their progress from time to time.

Extracurricular activities

The involvement of teachers in extracurricular activities is a great help in promoting a spirit of cooperation between the teachers and the students. It allows each to see and appreciate the other, in a more holistic, non-classroom context.

Commitment

Teachers will often make explicit commitments to their students. 'When you don't understand I'll go back. I want you to be here and to do well. When I see you trying, I will do my best to explain. It's only by our mistakes that we can learn. Don't put yourself down.' Such explicit statements do much to strengthen the relationship between teacher and student.

Be positive, look for what is right

How we react to student misbehaviour is determined by how we interpret and label it. If we try to put a positive construction on what we observe, it can really help in our relations with the students. For example, students who answer back may be seen as being cheeky but also as displaying courage. Those who argue with the teacher may, from another point of view, be displaying a developing sense of justice and independence of thought. Taking any piece of behaviour and deliberately interpreting it in a more positive way is known as 'positive reframing'. When we do this, we begin to recognise qualities in our students that we might otherwise miss. Once we see students in a positive light we tend to react more constructively to them.

Accept reality

To maintain credibility with a 'difficult' class, a teacher has to 'get real'. This involves among other things:

> *Examining critically the relevance of what you are trying to teach, and acknowledging honestly that some topics can be difficult and boring.*

Having realistic expectations of the students' abilities, based on their age, motivation (or lack of it), home backgrounds and culture, etc.

Allowing for the context of the class. The last lesson of the morning or the day is more difficult to teach. Anything unusual that breaks the routine or continuity of the school day, such as unusual weather conditions (snow), or the expected announcement of a 'half day' can adversely affect how students will behave in class. Sometimes a certain point is reached when it is better to face reality and let go of some of the normal expectations. We may have to concede that not very much work will be done on a particular day. In such circumstances it is foolish for a teacher to drive on, ignoring such factors. To try to grind students into working when the 'wind is blowing directly against you', undermines the teacher's authority and is destructive to his relationship with the students.

Accepting that the attention span of weak students is short; often not more than four minutes.

Accepting that the level of tidiness and organisation will be low.

Not expecting too high a standard. Many of the homes of difficult students are chaotic. Books will be forgotten or lost. Sometimes the teacher might be better off keeping all books and materials in school to avoid loss.

Avoid unnecessary complications

Some English teachers, for example, may wish to introduce a bit of variety into their lessons by teaching poetry on Mondays, the play on Tuesdays, the prescribed prose on Wednesdays and essay preparation on Thursdays. While this scheme might work with an organised class of keen students, it will only cause confusion in 'weak' classes. Expecting students to have a number of books in class every day, just in case they might be needed, will mean that some students will never get it right. For students in difficulty, classroom arrangements need to be kept simple and straightforward.

Homework

It is best to give a little, regularly. Negotiate reasonable levels of homework. Allow time to explain homework clearly. Always write instructions on the board and ensure students have time to write them down. Accept that in difficult classes some homework will always remain undone. Appreciate the difficulties some students have in working alone and the lack of a suitable, quiet place to study in some homes. Praise all efforts made. Give special attention to those requiring it.

When starting the lesson, work with those students who have the homework done. In this way you will be starting in a positive frame and making a bit of progress. Later during the lesson, the teacher can decide what to do with those students who didn't attempt the homework. Beware of the negativity generated in getting bogged down dealing with these students at the very beginning of the lesson. Teachers can easily end up frustrated. Getting involved in excuses is generally a waste of time and can be very draining on the teacher.

Manners and politeness

It cannot be assumed that all students know the appropriate behaviours involved in the life of a school. These may have to be taught. It is vital that the teacher is reasonable, fair, humane, consistent, predictable and treats all the students with the same degree of respect and fairness. Mutual respect should be the hallmark of all the interactions in the class. This concept of respect may have to be taught to students, who may be unfamiliar with it, and who may find it difficult to maintain a relationship with an adult that is not based on fear and antagonism.

Cultural differences between teachers and students can sometimes be an issue. Some 'deviant' behaviours and the use of slang or 'bad language', while unacceptable to teachers in a school context, may be quite acceptable in the student's own culture. Some students have to be taught to wait their turn, to listen to other people's points of view, even

if they disagree, not to shout down and interrupt others, to knock when entering a room, to tolerate and respect differences in others. Teaching the niceties of human interaction is every bit as important as the task of imparting a particular body of knowledge to students. Teachers can be over-attached to their plan to get the curriculum covered at all costs. From time to time, a teacher may need to move outside the subject area and deal with a real issue that is of concern to the students. The lesson may be subsidiary to the students' needs at a particular time and sometimes it may have to be abandoned altogether.

Listening

Listening to and negotiating with students can do a great deal to promote a positive class atmosphere. Give the students time to talk, and hear them out fully. Very often, the teacher needs to clarify what exactly students mean, as the possibilities for misunderstanding are great. 'Explain that to me again to make sure I understand you correctly. You will have to give me time to think about that. I need to check that with the head/your parents before we could consider…'. It is important in all these discussions that teachers are clear about their own boundaries, take the contributions of their students seriously, and keep the interaction at a professional level at all times. When we listen to students, we ought to do so as caring adults, trying to view things from their perspective, seeking to understand their struggles, and striving to help them honour their own feelings and experience of reality. When listening to students the employment of a specific listening skill, such as 'Following and Reflecting' (see pages 105–6) is very useful.

Listening carefully and being all 'palsy walsy' are not the same thing. Students, particularly difficult students, need direction and guidance. It is therefore remiss of any adult to ignore their own accumulated experience of life when entering into dialogue with students whose thinking and behaviour may not be constrained by the dictates of reason, a sense of responsibility or the cultural norms of society. Some teachers, youth leaders and parents treat young children as equals in the mistaken belief that they are respecting them. Ironically this is a disservice to young people, who neither have the emotional nor intellectual resources to relate to adults as equals or wish to do so.

Routine

When teaching difficult classes it is helpful if teachers begin and conduct the lesson in a predictable and routine manner. Whilst teaching, they can contribute to the smooth flow of the lesson by being consistent in their interactions with the students, clear in their instruction and unwavering in their resolve to follow through on agreed procedures and consequences. It is vital that teachers remain calm and professional at all times. Students with low self-esteem are particularly dependent on the routine, steadfastness and constancy of the teacher. School may be the only dependable routine in their daily lives and too much change can upset them.

◼ **Maintaining relationship with students**

Despite the best efforts of the teacher working with a difficult class, misbehaviour and conflict will inevitably arise. While it is imperative that the teacher confronts student misbehaviour, it is equally important that the teacher maintains a relationship with the errant student and with the class as a whole. Whenever a teacher has to act to confront persistent or serious misbehaviour, it is useful to check the following before deciding on a particular course of action:

What is my own role in the interactions with this student? Am I standing back from the situation sufficiently or am I getting 'hooked' personally?

Will the proposed action plan provide restitution to the injured party or teacher? Will the esteem of the injured party or teacher be restored? What effect will it have on the esteem of the miscreant?

Will the proposed action help the student take responsibility for his/her actions? Will the student learn that actions have natural consequences?

How damaging to the student–teacher relationship is the proposed action likely to be?

Will natural justice be done and be seen to be done?

What kind of (teacher/adult) behaviour are the students likely to see modelled in this interaction? If they witness and experience bullying and force used by their teachers, then we need not be surprised if that is the kind of behaviour they will resort to when they themselves are in conflict.

When faced with students who are difficult to control, poorly motivated, disobedient, defiant and very likely failing in school, what do teachers usually do? The following range of behaviours is typical of what teachers do:

criticise	sigh	reinforce
threaten	moralise	compliment
use sarcasm	personalise	encourage
isolate	disapprove	guide
punish	silence	question

The list on the left can be associated with coercive or punitive responses to student misbehaviour, while those on the right are more facilitatory in nature. We think it is fair to say that the 'natural' tendency of most teachers, when confronted with a class of difficult students is to lean towards the list on the left, i.e. to move into a punishing mode. Consider what effect this might have on students who are disaffected and have already taken on a rebellious role within the school system.

Punishments reinforce their negative view of school and drive them further away from their teachers. Trying to control and teach this class becomes a power struggle, an exhausting ordeal from the teacher's point of view. The students' behaviour improves, but only while they are being closely supervised and as long as the teacher 'sits on them'. The students work at a level just above the minimum of what they can get away with, but as soon as the teacher's back is turned, the messing about resumes.

In a school system that relies exclusively on strict punitive methods of control, the students see the teachers as the enemy. They will liken themselves to prisoners and view the teachers as warders. Any perceived 'weak link' among the teachers will be exploited mercilessly by the students. The lives of some teachers in that situation become hell. Their own colleagues, who often consider them to be the cause of the discipline problems in the first place, may even blame them.

When such a discipline system is failing in a school, the usual response of management and staff is to 'tighten up' on discipline, apply more and harder punishments, issue more report cards, have more detentions and exclusions. It is our belief, based on our years of working with difficult students, that such an approach to school discipline simply does not work. There is no improvement in student behaviour and the same students continue to cause trouble all the time, until they are finally excluded permanently from the school. Often a school discipline system, after operating a punitive regime for a few months, is saved from the consequences of operating in that manner by the arrival of the holidays.

In our view, teachers who work on building relationships with disaffected students, will have more success than those who rely exclusively on a punitive discipline system. We are not advocating a 'softly softly' approach when dealing with students who clearly have broken school rules. We acknowledge the necessity, in every school, of having and operating a Code of Discipline, as a support to the teachers and the students. However, it should be used like a police riot squad in a civil society; everybody knows it is there, but it is seldom visible on the streets, and is used only in emergencies. To keep the confrontational approach to the fore in a school or in any social system coarsens the working atmosphere and, in the long run, everyone suffers. In the next section we outline a strategy by which teachers can confront errant students, and effect a positive change in their behaviour, without punishing or humiliating them.

▧ Constructive confrontation

Given that humans are biologically programmed to compete for power and status, it is not surprising that confrontation is an inevitable part of our lives. It occurs in families, in politics, in business, in sport and very definitely in schools and classrooms.

Confrontation is an unavoidable part of the teaching dynamic, because if the teacher is not in control, the students will be. Teachers, therefore, need to be able to confront students in a way that minimises negativity and leaves them in a position where they can continue to command the respect of their students.

Constructive confrontation is a strategy for dealing with student misbehaviour that enables the teacher to manage the situation without having to resort to authoritarian or coercive methods. When executed correctly, it can be very effective in dealing with difficult students in a way that allows teachers to get what they want, while at the same time preserving the self-esteem of all concerned in the interaction.

It takes time and practice to appreciate the subtlety of this strategy and to get it right. The actual mechanics of the skill are simple enough to understand. However, the longer we have been applying it in classrooms, the more appreciative we are of its complexity and value. It demands of teachers that they be entuned to both their own feelings and those of their students. Neither of these requirements can be taken for granted. It also demands that when we enter into conflict we do so with an open mind about the eventual outcome; that we accept the fact that the student has ideas or feelings that need to be respected or heard, and that they have some control over the outcome. This requires that the teacher move outside the punishment/reward model that is dismissive of the person.

We offer this strategy to readers as another way of dealing with student misbehaviour, to complement but not replace their existing practice. Needless to say, it will not work with every student on every occasion.

There are six steps involved. Here we outline the essential features of each step and then take the reader through some case studies based on our own teaching experience.

Step 1: Stating the facts

The teacher begins by stating the facts in a clinical, non-evaluative, unemotional manner. A teacher might say something like 'Just now Martin, you said.....', or 'Thomas, you threw a piece of paper.' It is important that this statement merely states the bare objective facts of the matter, as a video camera might record the event. At first, this appears to be a simple thing to do but it is not as easy as it seems. Consider for example the following remarks made by teachers in response to student behaviour and decide whether they are statements of fact or not.

1. It is 9.12 a.m. and the lesson has started. Johnny enters the class-room. The teacher turns around and says

    'Johnny, you're late'

2. Mary contradicts the teacher and the teacher responds by saying

    'Mary, you're being cheeky'

3. Groups of students are laughing in the corner of the classroom. The teacher says

    'Stop sniggering, you lot over there'

4. Timmy is banging his ruler on the desk. The teacher says

    'Timmy, you are disrupting my class'

5. Paul kicks Alan's bag across the corridor. The teacher says to Paul

    'Just now you kicked Alan's bag across the corridor'

6. The teacher has corrected and graded Catherine's homework. When returning the homework the teacher says

    'Catherine, you could have made a greater effort and done a lot better than this'

Which of these six statements do you consider to be a statement of fact?

In the first case, '*Johnny, you're late*' is *not* a statement of fact. It is a value judgement made by the teacher. A dispassionate security camera would not record lateness. A non-evaluative statement of fact might go as follows: 'Johnny, it's 9.12 a.m. and you are coming into class now.' Note the difference in tone between the two statements. The use of the word 'late' in the first statement implies blame and may well provoke a hostile response. The second statement, on the other hand, is a state-ment of fact that cannot be refuted and is less likely to elicit a defensive response. Some readers may argue that 'Johnny, you're late' is a state-ment of fact but even if we allow this it cannot be denied that such a statement tends to set the stage for a negative exchange. Most teachers would find it provocative if their head confronted them in such a manner on the occasions when they are the ones who are late.

The second example '*Mary, you are being cheeky*' is clearly judge-mental. A statement of fact could be 'Mary, just now you said.....', repeating exactly what Mary said.

In the third example, 'You appear to be amused' might be a more accurate statement of fact than '*Stop sniggering you lot over there*'. The use of words like sniggering or smirking is likely to stir up resentment or anger. In the same way '*Timmy, you are making a noise tapping your ruler on the desk*', is an example of a statement of fact which might apply in the fourth case, as opposed to the highly evaluative comment '*Timmy, you are disrupting my class*'. The fifth sentence, '*Just now you kicked Alan's bag across the corridor*' is the only statement of fact on the list when you apply the sharp focus that is required to employ this strategy correctly. In the last case 'Catherine, in your homework assign-ment you completed Questions 1 and half of Question 3' is a statement of fact that cannot be disputed. Unlike the one we give in example six above, it does not put the student down.

In ordinary circumstances, some of the original six statements qualify as statements of fact, but in the volatile atmosphere of teacher–student interaction, they can set the exchange off on the wrong foot from the beginning. A bald judgement such as 'You're late' can trigger hostility and resentment, leading to what teachers refer to as 'cheek'. The student might answer smartly 'No! I'm not late. The head told me to pick up the papers in the corridor, before I went to class.'

It is very easy to get Step 1 wrong. The statement of fact must be expressed in such a manner that it cannot be refuted. At this stage fault finding and judging are unhelpful. The object of Step 1 is simply to allow the teacher and the student to agree about what happened. This helps both teacher and student to avoid getting caught up in a web of confusion, defensiveness or denial that often has little to do with the incident involved.

It is not necessary to be as tentative as this all the time in our inter-actions with students. The care and sensitivity we are asking for just now are particular to Step 1 of what we call constructive confrontation. It is important because it maximises our chances of achieving the opti-mum outcome.

Step 2: What I feel

At this point the teacher shares his feelings (regarding the behaviour described in Step 1) directly with the student involved.

In this step, an honest and direct expression of feelings tends to humanise the exchange and enhances the possibilities of a positive outcome. If we can say 'John, you are tapping your pen on the table and I'm becoming frustrated', we are more likely to make meaningful contact with the student than if we begin in a manner such as 'John, have you any consideration for others?'

Many teachers fear that they are giving their power away if they share their feelings with students. They feel that this kind of disclosure is likely to diminish their authority. Ironically, the converse is true. Contrary to what one might expect, our experience, and that of other teachers, suggest that such disclosure is a very powerful strategy when dealing with difficult students.

Disclosure of feelings can often be difficult because it is not easy to express accurately what we are feeling at a particular point in time. Sometimes when we feel sad and vulnerable we make jokes or laugh. When we feel insecure and afraid we sometimes try to regain power and control by aggressively displaying anger.

Feelings like irritation, annoyance, anger, outrage are, in effect, 'secondary' feelings. On reflection, it is very likely that such feelings are a reaction to more 'primary' feelings like frustration, sadness, anxiety, exhaustion, fear, or embarrassment. Primary feelings, when shared, tend to bring people closer together because they establish a common bond, even in the most unlikely circumstances. On the other hand, secondary feelings divide us and may set the scene for conflict. They imply an element of blaming and can give rise to defensiveness and resistance in the student. See Appendix 2 for more examples of primary and secondary feelings. When in a confrontation with another, the sharing of any feeling will have a humanising influence, especially when employed in this technique.

Step 3: Why I feel

The third step in a constructive confrontation is to reveal to the student the tangible effect his behaviour is having on the teacher or the other students in the class. The word 'because' is invariably used. The teacher points out to the student that his actions have negative consequences. If, for example, a student is talking in class and we confront him in terms of some rule, he is less likely to cooperate than if we can show him, in a non-blaming way, how his behaviour is negatively affecting us, in some practical way. The tangible effect of a student talking might be that the teacher could not concentrate on a difficult piece of work. Students resent the imposition of school rules if they feel that it is just teachers bossing them about and no more.

Step 4: We have a problem

The fourth step is simply a clear statement that 'We have a problem here and we need to work together to find a solution that we can all agree on.'

Step 5: Silence

This can be difficult for the teacher to maintain but it allows the student to make an input to the discussion, at this point, if they want to. They may need to vent their feelings and it is helpful to allow them to do so. However, the teacher must not be sidetracked and must keep the focus on the common goal of finding a solution to this shared problem.

Step 6: What plan can we make to fix the problem?

This final step involves working out with the student a solution to the problem. This may involve an apology and such action that will make restitution for any damage caused. It may involve defining exactly what is required of everyone.

The teacher should hold back from telling the student what needs to be done. It is better if the student offers suggestions as to how the problem can be solved to everyone's satisfaction. He may need help in realising the extent of the problem he has caused and the lengths he has to go to fix it. When negotiating with the student the teacher should not settle for half measures or accept the first offer the student makes. 'I wouldn't be entirely satisfied with that' is a useful phrase to use when, for example, the teacher wants the student to go further than merely to agree to apologise for his behaviour. In fact, apologies are of little value, unless they come spontaneously from students who are really clear about the difficulties they are causing and are taking responsibility for their part.

Students who break school or class rules need to be confronted regularly, on the basis that they are infringing the rights of others. They may need to learn a better way of behaving that will meet their own needs. This is time-consuming, but it is real education and, in reality, is no more energy sapping or depressing than chasing around after these students with report cards, detention notes and punishment slips.

Case Study 1

It is 3.35 p.m. on a sunny Friday afternoon in May. Mr O'Keeffe is teaching maths to Class 5.3 as their final lesson of the day. It is his seventh class that day. Despite being tired, he is trying to explain a difficult concept to the students. On turning from the board, he observes Jim Murphy throwing a balled-up piece of paper at Timmy Scanlon.

What options are open to Mr O'Keeffe?

What would you do in that situation?

There are a wide range of responses open to a teacher, ranging from ignoring the incident, to sending Jim Murphy to the year head. How a teacher will respond to an incident is a function of many variables such as the time of day, the academic expectations of the students, the normative behaviour of the class, or how the teacher is feeling at the time. A constructive confrontation might go as follows:

Step 1: 'Just now, Jim, you threw a piece of paper across the room.'

Step 2: 'I feel frustrated…' [note use of primary feeling]

Step 3: '…because I'm trying to get this piece of work finished so we can all get out of here on time.'

Step 4: 'Jim, we have a problem here.'

Step 5: Silence.

In this actual case, used to illustrate the technique, there was no need to go to Step 6 because without being asked to do so Jim got up from his seat, walked to the back of the class, picked up the paper, put it in the bin and returned to his seat. The lesson continued without further incident.

This student, incidentally, had a proven record of being difficult to manage. Mr O'Keeffe noted that he had been 'pleasantly surprised' by the student's response.

Case Study 2

A young, female, temporary teacher was teaching geography to a class of Year 11 boys. She had completed a piece of work on the board and asked the students to copy it down into their books. The teacher stood aside but was still blocking the view of one rather tough-looking, 16-year-old student, who called out in front of the class, 'Move your ass!' The teacher was completely disconcerted and didn't quite know what to do. The bell signalling the end of class sounded and she left the room upset.

Later in the staffroom, when she had recovered somewhat, she wrote out a Report Card on the incident, but realised that the full import of what had happened was not conveyed in print. She feared that the head would not understand the full significance of the incident; that he might conclude that she could not handle the class and that she might end up in a worse situation. She decided to try a constructive confrontation with the student. If that failed, she felt she could still fall back on the disciplinary report card system of the school. She spent some time preparing what she would say. She reflected on how she was feeling and what strategies she might employ to secure a satisfactory outcome. She located the class on the timetable, went to their classroom and with the teacher's permission she called the student outside. The constructive confrontation went as follows:

Step 1: The facts of the matter were clear enough: 'Towards the end of my class you called out "Move your ass".'

Step 2: The teacher had originally thought of saying 'I am angry about this', but on reflection she realised that deep down she feared that if she let this comment, with its sexual innuendo, go unchallenged, there was no telling where it would lead to. She said, 'I felt afraid when you said that...'

Step 3: '...because I feel that if I let a remark like that go, students will take it that it's OK to say things like that, or even worse.' The student interjected that he didn't mean anything by it and it was 'just a joke'.

Step 4: The teacher accepted that he was not aware of the full implications of his remark but she insisted that 'We have a problem here.'

Step 5: In this case, there was no need for silence because the student had already accepted that there was a problem.

Step 6: The student offered his apologies for any hurt caused. The teacher thanked him but said that she wouldn't really be satisfied with that. After some discussion, the student offered to apologise, in front of the class, at the start of her next lesson. The teacher checked if he would be able to do this, indicating that she felt it would take courage to do so and that she would not like him to do that if he could not do it sincerely. He said that he could handle it maturely and they agreed on a format. The next day the student stood up and apologised to the teacher in front of the class. The teacher thanked him and commended him for doing so. She then took the opportunity to explain to this class of boys what it felt like to be at the receiving end of such comments, and spent a little time on the subject of sexual harassment. The class then proceeded as normal.

How do we evaluate any method of dealing with teacher–student conflict? How can we judge the success or otherwise of any teacher intervention when a confrontation takes place? The following criteria are useful in assessing the success of an intervention:

1. *Behaviour.* Is the student's misbehaviour likely to stop? If it had been a regular occurrence in the past, is the frequency of the student's misbehaviour likely to be reduced?

2. *Self-Esteem.* Has the self-esteem of the student been raised as a result of the interaction with the teacher? Will the self-esteem of the teacher, as a professional, be improved as a result of the interaction with the student(s)?

3. *Relationship.* Has the student–teacher relationship improved as a result of the confrontation? Will the teacher's relationship with the whole class be better after the constructive confrontation? Will there be a more positive, respectful, cooperative atmosphere in the classroom afterwards?

4. *Class atmosphere.* Will the level of student negativity towards teachers and the school system be reduced?

5. *Responsibility.* Will the level of the students' responsibility for their own actions be increased?

6. *Modelling.* In the interaction, is the teacher modelling an acceptable way of relating in life?

When teachers are asked to assess the outcome of the second case study in terms of these criteria, they tend to agree on a number of things. They feel that the student is unlikely to repeat that kind of behaviour. Secondly, they feel that because of the sensitive handling of the situation and the teacher's praising of the student's response, it is likely that his self-esteem will increase. The same can be said in relation to the teacher who has successfully managed the incident herself. It is also felt that the teacher–student relationship will improve and that the whole class will be more positive than if he had been punished. Similarly, it is felt that the students will be more willing to take responsibility for their actions in this kind of emotional climate. Finally, most agree that the handling of this case models a positive way of dealing with relationship difficulties, in a general sense.

Later, when she thought about it, the teacher noted how different the outcomes were between constructive confrontation and resorting to the disciplinary code of the school. She felt that by using the constructive confrontation method some real education had taken place. The relationship between her and the boys had improved and it was unlikely that a further incident of that nature would occur. If she had resorted to the school discipline system and reported the student to the year head, the student, bearing in mind his record, would have been given a fixed-term exclusion. He would have learned nothing and would have availed himself of the first opportunity to act up in her class in order to get even. The teacher's relationship with the class would have deteriorated and her difficulties in teaching them increased.

We cannot emphasise enough that constructive confrontation is a subtle technique that requires practice. When learning to play golf, a minute incorrect inflexion can send the ball flying off into the rough. So too in this technique; it is easy to get it wrong, particularly in step 1, by setting an accusatory tone. From start to finish the whole approach needs to be strong, while remaining tentative and flexible, as opposed to being rigidly used as a tool for manipulation.

As we said at the beginning of this section, constructive confrontation does not always work. The whole approach can become a mockery, in the hands of insensitive people. It will not work in a hostile atmosphere, where there is a negative relationship between the teacher and the students. Sceptical readers can dream up any number of impossible 'what if' situations for which the strategy will not work. Teachers who are heavily invested in the authoritarian mode of relating to students, for example, are unlikely to succeed in applying constructive confrontation. Our experience is that it is a very useful method of confronting difficult students and of getting them on your side without the use of coercive methods that inevitably lead to more difficulties for all involved.

■ You're not listening to me!

Some teachers maintain that students are being listened to too much and that if the students sat down, shut up and did what they were told everything would be alright. In reality, this is not a long-term option because when students feel that they have not been 'heard' they become less motivated, less involved, less cooperative, sometimes hostile and in extreme cases, destructive. The teachers then spend excessive amounts of time and energy pushing, checking, monitoring, punishing, and generally chasing after students.

Students have been known to complain that their teachers don't listen to them; yet the teachers insist that they do. Very often, however, they are trying to hear students in the rushed moments between classes or during the lesson, when the greater part of a teacher's energy is focused on keeping the class under control and working.

An obvious element in any conflict resolution process is the clarity of the communication that takes place between the parties involved. When teachers and students interact, misunderstandings can easily arise because the participants are not listening to each other. The kind of listening we are referring to here is a professional skill that teachers employ for a specific purpose. It is used in order that students will feel 'heard' and understood. This in turn will help to reduce the possibility of misunderstandings occurring and negativity arising. Intelligent and empathic listening by teachers humanises their interaction with students. It enables the students to become aware of what is 'going on for them' and what options are open to them. It enables them to make the best choice for themselves. A culture of listening in a school ensures good communication between students and teachers and reduces the context for any disruptive, irresponsible behaviour.

Often when we think we are listening what we are actually doing is formulating our next response or question. Instead of listening to a student, teachers often become preoccupied by internal responses which may block concentration and interfere with their ability to receive the student's messages. Typical distractions include:

■ Thinking about what to say, when it's my turn to say something.

■ Analysing the student's motives.

■ Thinking about how the student should solve his problem.

■ Planning the advice I will give.

■ Thinking of ways of cheering up the student.

The most important listening response takes place inside the listener's head. This involves focusing full attention on the speaker, concentrating on what the speaker is saying, and experiencing what is being talked about from the speaker's perspective. A good listener hears not only the words, but also the feeling(s) behind the words. He receives the messages communicated through tone of voice, facial expression, and other body language. The effective listener's whole focus is on understanding the total message being communicated to him, rather than analysing or evaluating the problem. There are a number of observable responses that are characteristic of an effective listener. Here we focus on two: Following and Reflecting.

'Following' responses occur when the listener is attentively absorbing the information being communicated. You are following what the speaker is saying and you indicate this by non-verbal means such as nodding your head, leaning slightly towards the speaker, or by using brief expressions ('Yes', 'I see', 'Really!') that communicate your interest. Your questions should be confined to seeking information that is essential to following and understanding.

'Reflecting' responses encourage the speaker to feel understood, to express feelings, to get to the root of the problem, and sometimes to find the solution for himself. They also help the listener to concentrate on what is being said. Reflecting responses involve either:

(a) reflecting the feelings communicated by the speaker. 'That must have been very difficult for you.' 'I can see that you are angry.' 'You're worried about that.'

or

(b) paraphrasing the content of what the speaker has said. 'Just a minute John, let me see if I understand you correctly. Your concern is that.....'

or

(c) repeating the last word the speaker used. This surprisingly simple tactic assures the speaker that you are 'with them' and encourages them to go on.

The following account, of a teacher at a large secondary school, illustrates the use of these three listening skills.

Mary's story

It was 4.15 p.m. on a Friday and I was about to go home when Alice, one of my Year 8 pupils, appeared at my classroom door. She glanced down the corridor and assured, perhaps by its emptiness, fixed her gaze on me. With a touch of defiance and a good measure of anger she blurted out, 'Miss, I'm leaving.'

My habitual response to a situation like this would have been to say things like 'What's the matter? Do you want to talk about it?' or 'You don't really want to leave school do you?' or 'You're upset. Don't make any rash decision until you have calmed down.' As it was after last class on a Friday, I was even tempted to arrange an appointment with the school counseller for the following Monday morning so that Alice could speak to him and deal with her problem then. Then I remembered something I had been reading about listening. The suggestion was that when dealing with students who are unhappy teachers should just repeat the last word they heard the student say, and then wait for more.

Here stood Alice at my door and she was leaving school.

'You're going to leave,' I said.

'I'm gonna leave ...I can't take it no more.'

'You can't take it any more.'

'My mother says I can leave 'cause it's doin' her head in; me coming home every day all screwed up. She says it's not worth it.'

Tears started to well up in her eyes.

'You go home every day all upset.'

'It's the way I'm being treated here.'

'It's the way you're being treated in school.'

I thought to myself, she's going to catch on to what I'm doing, and then she'll go ballistic. But, she didn't. I found that I really didn't need to say very much at all but to follow what Alice was saying or to reflect back to her what she was feeling.

'They're all making fun of me, Miss.'

'They're all making fun of you. That must be very difficult for you.'

*'Yes Miss. They keep calling me a *****'*

*'They called you a *****'*

'Last Friday Miss, in the Food Tech room, they were ...'

She went on and on for some time, pouring out the causes – real or imagined – of her hurt, anger and misery. By all appearances, she left my classroom feeling the same as she did when she came in. That was a real disappointment to me. It seemed as if I had not done anything to help her.

The weekend came and I forgot about Alice until the following Wednesday, when I bumped into her tutor in the corridor. Feeling a little guilty at not having followed it up on the Monday, I asked tentatively 'How are things going with Alice?'

'Fine. Funny you should ask. She was causing a lot of trouble lately and said that she was going to leave school but she seems to have settled down this week. I don't know what happened but she has changed.'

The change in Alice was dramatic: she stayed on to finish her GCSEs. This experience illustrates a valuable lesson in listening. When all we can do is listen, we are doing a lot.

■ Motivation

All behaviour is purposeful.　W. Glasser.

The rewarding and punishing of children seem to be the major concept of motivation to have been tried in English education, since the days of payment by results in the late nineteenth century. Even today, what many teachers want most are new techniques that will enable them to force students to do their bidding. In the performance table climate that dominates education, a simple fact goes unnoticed. Students work when they want to.

In order to teach young people with any degree of success, it is necessary that teachers consider what motivates students to do anything at all. One way of looking at this question, that we have found useful in our teaching, is that proposed by William Glasser, the founder of the Institute of Reality Therapy in Los Angeles and author of many books on psychology, mental health and education. Glasser rejects the Stimulus–Response theory that has dominated educational thinking for over a century, and does not accept the notion that human behaviour is governed by external reward and punishment.

Glasser suggests that apart from the basic survival needs of air, water, food and shelter, there are four other needs that all humans strive to satisfy, whenever they do anything. These needs are to have 'Fun', to experience 'Freedom', to have a sense of 'Power or Status' in their lives and to feel 'Loved or a sense of Belonging'. In his books *Control Theory, Schools Without Failure* and *Control Theory in the Classroom* (see References). Glasser argues that all human behaviour constitutes an attempt, on the part of the individual, to satisfy one of these four basic needs.

We have found Glasser's ideas to be of enormous value in our own teaching work. Obviously some fun, or even the possibility of it, can really change the atmosphere in a classroom. Similarly, whenever students are given choices (freedom), as opposed to directives, the level of cooperation increases. If students are experiencing success in class, their power need is being served and they will respond positively to the teacher. When students feel valued as people of importance, to be spoken to with respect (as opposed to being ordered about), the context for misbehaviour and disruption is dissolved and ceases to make sense to the students themselves. If, on the other hand, students feel put down or criticised, then incidents of indiscipline increase as they seek to satisfy their power/status need by inappropriate means.

Teachers who use Glasser's ideas focus consciously on these four needs when building a relationship with their students, and through that relationship they model appropriate behaviour and set limits. These teachers find that discipline problems are less frequent and tend to dissolve at source, rather than having to be solved by punitive action.

Glasser also speaks of the 'pictures' people have in their minds, that they believe will satisfy the needs they have, at a particular time. A student might be motivated to study physics by a picture they have of themselves working as a highly paid engineer in charge of a huge project at some time in the future. When students have such a picture and can relate school activity to the realisation of its implied goals, they will be self-motivated. Experiencing success in school enhances the student's sense of power and status, and is in itself need fulfilling.

The converse is also true. When students habitually experience failure they lose all sense of motivation and stop trying, in order to insulate themselves from pain of failure and the resultant damage to their sense of power and self worth.

In the exam-led, results-driven culture of education, the motivation of students, who are not performing well or are not keeping up with the best of them, is constantly being undermined. Given the realities of modern society it may well be that this is inevitable but the damage can be minimised if there are good relations between such students and their teachers. If the teacher can maintain a strong bond with students, they will continue to make an effort and hopefully do justice to their own potential. By setting these students achievable tasks and getting them to successfully 'jump low fences', teachers can implant a picture of success in their students' minds so that they may then be encouraged to attempt more difficult work. Experiencing success satisfies a student's power need. In due course the student may be self-motivated to learn because he has made the connection between power and knowledge.

When working with students, and particularly with those experiencing difficulties, the most destructive behaviours, in terms of relationship, are criticism and punishment. While they may appear to work in the short term, in the long run people who rely on this approach forfeit any real control over the situation. In schools, some teachers, because of the force of their personality, can continue to bully students into obeying them. However, punishment and criticism do not ultimately enhance the students' sense of responsibility or motivation, even though it may appear to work for some.

All students, particularly those with low self-esteem, have an instinctive negative reflex to criticism. This presents the teacher with a particular difficulty, since correcting students' work and their behaviour is an integral part of the job. Glasser suggests that the teachers get students to make value judgements about their own work/behaviour: 'What do you think of this work yourself?' or 'Is what you are doing

OK?' Glasser believes that the making of value judgements by the student about his own behaviour is necessary if he is to change that behaviour. This approach is in sharp contrast to the prevailing situation where the teacher makes the value judgements for the students, who feel 'put down' in the process.

We can now address the question of motivation by asking ourselves when will students start applying themselves to study? We feel the answer includes some of the following ideas:

■ When the activity promises to fulfil a need (Fun, Power, Love, Freedom).

■ The activity itself must be need-satisfying.

■ When there is a realistic chance of success.

■ When there is a good relationship between the teacher and the student. When the student feels safe to try, i.e. trusts the teacher that there will not be any punishing or criticism for mistakes made.

When parents ask 'How can I make him study?', the answer is 'You can't.' However, students will study when:

■ they are set realistic goals;

■ given a reasonable chance of success;

■ they have a home environment conducive to study;

■ they are unobtrusively supported;

■ and then left alone to get on with it.

You can't make people do anything for very long, unless they find something in it for themselves. When difficulties arise the place to start working is on the relationship.

■ Some characteristic traits of children from troubled homes

In an ideal family children are provided with the things that they need to develop their potentialities fully. There is mutual respect and love shown by the parents for each other. They communicate honestly and openly, and generally reach agreement on how things are to be organised, such that life does not become an empty, unsatisfying, exhausting struggle. Generally, they have a common considered approach to the rearing of their children, who are given independence and freedom commensurate with their age. Traditionally, the functional family is hierarchical. It matters little whether it is patriarchal or matriarchal, as long as decisions are taken in a caring way that balance the needs of all concerned. We all know that this ideal is not easily achieved and most of us struggle to do the best we can.

A family is said to be dysfunctional when the struggle within the family itself begins to absorb an inordinate amount of emotional and physical energy. This results in family members being drained, angry, frustrated, hurt or deeply unhappy. There are many possible reasons for dysfunction in families but, whatever the root cause of the dysfunction may be, common recognisable symptoms emerge.

Our aim here is to draw the attention of teachers to the manifestation of these symptoms so that they may become more understanding and accepting of the children in their care. It may also help them to devise strategies that can keep their contact with students meaningful and growthful. It helps when teachers have some awareness of their own 'dysfunction' from their own family experience, as this enables them to be more sympathetic and understanding, as opposed to being condescending, patronising and intolerant.

At the core of the problem, from the point of view of the children in such families, is the emotional unavailability and insensitivity of their parents.

In the case of families where addiction is presenting a problem, the 'addict' is totally preoccupied with the focus of their addiction; their co-dependent partner is not fully available either, because of their own inadequacies and their preoccupation with the addict's activities. Often the 'addiction' is shared. The addict 'uses' to help them stay away from the pain of being present in the here and now. What they use can take many forms: alcohol, drugs, sport, religion, sex, work, career; the possibilities are endless. Parents may not be 'present' or available to their children for many other reasons also. These might include things like poverty, physical or mental ill health, bereavement, separation or the emotionally crippling residue of neglect, violence or abuse in their own childhood. The children indulge in whatever strategies they can employ to gain love and approval, have their needs met and try to hold the family system together.

The following model of dysfunctional family systems was developed originally from the observations of addiction counsellors working with families that had suffered from alcoholism. It was found that in troubled families children tended to respond in certain typical ways and to take on one of four roles within the family system. The family roles that tend to emerge are that of the hero, the scapegoat, the lost child and the clown. Each, as we shall see, fulfils certain requirements in the family.

Children develop a dominant role. They carry that role into the classroom. Later, as adults, they will carry that role into their work and life. In certain circumstances it is possible that during their childhood some children may get an opportunity to play a number of different roles as the configuration of their family changes.

Teachers in school often notice that one child in a troubled family turns out to be 'marvellous'. This is the *hero*, the 'little mother of the family' or 'the little man about the house', who always does what is right. Heroes are driven people. In school they work hard, are high achievers, getting good grades relative to their ability. Though organised and efficient, they tend to be rigid and anxious in their studies.

They have to be right all the time. They are often very competitive at sport and readily engage in extracurricular activities. Heroes are very responsible and are often regarded as 'ideal' students by their teachers. Socially they are constantly on the go. They cannot stop. Their lives are full of 'I must.....', 'I have to.....' and 'I should.....'. Heroes are popular with their friends but are needy of approval. The role of the hero is to provide self-worth to the family. Someone they can be proud of; someone, who despite all the other difficulties, appears to be getting on.

Behind the 'success', the hero feels inadequate and anxious. Life is lacking in real fun. Work is their way of keeping feelings at bay. As an adult without awareness, self-acceptance and self-esteem, they may become workaholics living driven, joyless lives. They often exhibit an inordinate need to be in control. They tend to be a perfectionist, who in extreme cases can become manipulative and neurotic. They often marry a dependent person and thus, in time, graduate into the role of a co-dependent spouse. Teachers can play a significant part in helping heroes celebrate their strengths, while at the same time releasing themselves from the stress associated with their self-enforced role.

In the same family, another child may emerge as a rebellious troublemaker. The *scapegoat* comes across as either hostile, defiant and angry, or resentful, withdrawn and sullen. At school, they quickly come to the attention of teachers because of their insolence or uncontrolled temper outbursts. Though they may be intelligent, they do not apply themselves to their studies and frequently do not achieve anything like their full potential in school. Teachers may wonder 'Why can't you be like your (hero) brother/sister?'

Underneath the tough exterior, the scapegoat feels hurt, rejected and inadequate. He has very low self-esteem. In the dysfunctional family system, the scapegoat tends to get blamed for everything. They take the focus away from the real problem and provide a series of cathartic crises, which permit the parents to join in a common cause, trying to cope with all the trouble they precipitate. 'Look what you have done now. You're excluded from school yet again. Your father and I are so worried. We don't know what to do with you.'

One way that teachers can help scapegoats is by recognising and redirecting their courage and leadership abilities. It is surprising how often troublemakers, if given responsibility by the teacher, will respond positively to the trust placed in them.

Some children in difficult family situations simply get lost, withdraw and become loners. This is the *lost child*. They cope with the family's problems by shutting them out of their own little world. They have few, if any, friends. Teachers experience them as 'spaced out', daydreamers, solitary, shy and withdrawn. In class they present no problems and can easily be overlooked by teachers, who are preoccupied with other more demanding students. They are so quiet that when they are absent from school the teacher might not even notice. The lost child often feels lonely and unimportant. They tend to be passive, have no opinion of their own on anything and display little zest for life. They have difficulty asserting themselves, are indecisive and prefer to acquiesce with others, rather than state their own preferences. In relationships, this leaves them vulnerable. With help, they can become independent, and express the creativity and imagination that is a strong part of their personality.

The final role that children play in troubled families is that of the *clown*. They cope with the family's problems by being super cute and immature. Clowns tend to be hyperactive, anxious, with a short attention span and frequently have learning difficulties. They appear to be constantly on the verge of hysterics, are terrified of being alone, and often feel inadequate or unimportant. Their role in the family is to provide comic relief and humour when things get tense. In school, teachers find them giddy and hard to reach because of the compulsive nature of the clowning. They can find it impossible to 'get off the stage'.

Behind the role they are fragile, immature and insecure. With help, their energy and humour can be seen as a valuable social asset, once they can release themselves from the role that has worked for them in the limiting circumstances of the family.

There is, of course, no pure form of these family roles and individual students may exhibit traits that are a mixture of the different roles. The roles within a family can also change. If, for example, the hero grows up and leaves the family home, then a younger child will change roles and assume the tasks of the absent hero.

This description of dysfunctional family roles is a crude approximation that can at best only provide the teacher with some clue as to what is going on for a child. Despite its drawbacks, it does alert the teacher to the fact that these children are not 'bad' but rather that they are in trouble and in need of help and guidance.

What can teachers do?

The first step is to recognise and accept the student as they are, in whatever role they appear to play. Schools tend to unduly reward heroes for their diligence and the lost children because they are no bother. Scapegoats and clowns also need to be valued for the contribution they make to the class group. The courage and honesty of the scapegoat can be honoured just as much as the 'head down' application of the hero. The humour and energy of the clown, though challenging to teachers, are more enlivening than the passivity of the lost child.

Secondly, teachers need to look beyond the visible role and see the vulnerable hurt of the individual behind the mask. Teachers can help the student to move out of role. For example, they might, in a sensitive way, encourage the hero to lighten up, to give herself time for leisure, or recommend that she relax and not feel that she is responsible for everything. We can watch out for opportunities to involve the lost child in group activities. The clown needs to be taken seriously: 'Tom, that's really funny but I think you are also telling me something serious that is important to you.' Whenever the teacher has to organise the class for some activity, the leadership skills of the scapegoat can be harnessed to help the teacher and in doing so entrust the scapegoat with responsibility.

Finally, as teachers, we can help these students by being as honest as possible about our own feelings when working with students. In doing so, we model responsible ways of dealing with emotions such as anger or disappointment.

When students enjoy relationships where there is a high degree of acceptance and respect, where there is honesty and openness about feelings, and where they feel understood, they tend to forsake defensive roles of their own accord. Whenever we manage to establish this kind of relationship we become more than instructors. We become teachers.

■ Strategies 'low achievers' use for coping with school

'Switched off and spaced out'

In 1996, we conducted an informal survey of low-achieving Year 8 students, in a secondary school, to ascertain their attitudes to, and expectations of, school. The students, members of the 'lowest' class in a streamed system, had proven to be particularly difficult to teach and many members of the class had a history of indiscipline, exclusion and truancy. The aim of the survey was to try to ascertain their level of awareness and their ideas concerning the underlying reasons for their disruptive behaviour.

When interviewed, the students professed that they wanted to learn, to do well, to pass their exams, to get on with their teachers and to have some fun. These responses surprised many of their teachers who pointed out that the behaviour of these students would not have evinced any interest on their part in attempting to achieve these objectives.

When asked to reflect on what they found unpleasant about school, the students listed the following as being particularly difficult to cope with:

■ Being expected to maintain total silence for long periods of time.

■ Reading, especially being asked to read aloud which they frequently found embarrassing.

■ The whole class being blamed for the misbehavior of a few and subsequently being punished as a group.

■ Not getting a chance to give their point of view.

■ Being very bored for much of their time in school.

■ Not being able to understand the material being taught.

■ Living under threat of (inevitable) punishment.

■ Giving incorrect responses to teachers' questions and being shown up in front of the whole class.

■ Getting too much homework, not having it done and not knowing how to do it.

■ Being made fun of by other students.

■ Being bullied all the time by their own peers. Constant pressure to conform to the group.

■ Feeling uncared for by the teachers and the school system generally.

It was clear that for many of these students the school experience was one of constant frustration and failure, resulting in unsatisfactory relationships with many of their teachers. They experienced constant negative correction from teachers and were made fun of by able classmates. School was a hassle for them, all the time. A battleground!

In situations like this, the teachers are caught in a double bind, with a curriculum to teach and a large class to prepare for exams. If they do not hassle and push, work will grind to a halt and students will fail their exams.

Even with the best will in the world, a subject teacher can find it virtually impossible to give approval to students who are constantly underachieving. Teachers point out that they have virtually no time available to devote to helping individuals and, in any case, individuals tended to be resistant to that kind of attention. The whole context is conducive to endless conflict, recrimination, disillusionment and 'burn out'.

What effect does this experience have on these students?

When children are put into the 'bottom' class, they resent it. It damages their motivation and attitude towards school. No matter what attempts are made by school authorities to disguise the streamed nature of the system, the students have no difficulty in recognising their situation, whatever their class is called. The same is true, of course, for students who fail the Eleven Plus and go to 'wide ability' or 'high' schools.

The effect on them is a gradual, slow but steady erosion of self-esteem, confidence, motivation and ambition. In time there develops among this group of students a 'delinquent subculture' (Hargreaves *et al.* 1975), where these students will misbehave, in order to satisfy their need for power, fun, freedom and belonging.

Students are well aware of the behaviours they choose in order to survive in these circumstances. As individuals, they resent the situation and are critical of the teachers who are unable to control them. As a class group, however, they seem to be unable to control themselves and to do anything to stop the part they play in the general fooling around. In such circumstances, it is often the individuals who are emotionally damaged and lack any sense of responsibility, who dominate the class. The following are some of the behaviours that students consciously employ in an effort to reduce the pain of being in school.

Some keep trying to understand what the teacher is doing in class and this often ends in frustration and anger when the students are continually faced with their own inability to comprehend the lesson. Others give up. The few, who can afford to, get private tutors.

Some switch off and drop out; day-dream in class; keep quiet...and (they hope) remain unnoticed. Some draw pictures or doodle in their book. Some do not even try to participate in class; do not attempt to do the homework, or copy if necessary.

Some students deliberately introduce confusion into classwork by seeking to involve the teacher in their problems. They might announce for example 'Miss, my book got lost.' They deliberately 'forget' text-book or materials. They make meaningless time-wasting excuses like 'I can't write Miss, my pen's run out.' They exploit the teacher's own insecurity and forgetfulness by insisting, for example, that the teacher never gave them homework to do or pretending that they handed it in last Friday. In fact, they will do anything that will prevent the teacher proceeding with classwork.

Some rebel and 'have a laugh', or show overt signs of boredom by yawning, sighing, humming, fidgeting or making clicking sounds to annoy the teacher. Some will try moving to a different seat and start talking to their friends during class. Others will try to 'take the teacher down' by playing up, joking, making fun of and baiting the teacher. The aim is to seize every opportunity to disrupt the class.

Another ploy is to 'escape' to the toilet or lockers, or better still 'go on the hop' and truant from school altogether.

Sometimes they will collectively decide not to cooperate with the teacher. 'Let's go on strike. Nobody is to answer any questions. Don't put your hand up.' In that situation they will make fun of and intimidate any classmate who responds to the teacher's questions, by hissing 'SSSSSwot' at them until they stop.

Some feign interest by asking 'pretend' questions of the teachers or try to distract them from the lesson plan by asking irrelevant questions like 'Sir, what year was President Kennedy shot?' Just as the teacher has got the class settled, and is ready to begin the lesson, a student will put his hand up and ask 'Sir, what's the Milky Way?' or 'Miss, is there a parent–teacher meeting next Thursday?', or any question to prevent the teacher getting work started.

Students, irrespective of ability, have the same fundamental needs. These include the need to succeed, i.e. to get things right, to belong to a group, to have a sense of achievement and satisfaction in their work, to have some hope in a future, to receive affirmation and praise and to have some fun. When low achieving students do not find satisfaction in the normal learning activities of the classroom, then they resort to disruptive measures to get their buzz.

Many students who present difficulties in class act in a totally self-centred (not necessarily selfish) manner in response to very immediate needs of their own. They are unconcerned about the long-term consequences of their actions and are often in a condition of minimal self-awareness or even denial. They do not want to be contacted in that place by well-meaning adults who seek to 'infect them' with the responsibilities and obligations of adult life. They want the adults to 'draw the line', to be in charge, to do all the thinking and to carry the responsibility for what is going on, thus allowing them to get on with being children.

Any teacher who crosses the line unprepared and who pleads with these students to respect them, and to be fair and considerate to one another, will be punished severely by the students for what they perceive as naivety and weakness.

Dysfunctional, troublesome students can be merciless in their abuse of teachers. They constantly push the limits as far as they dare and in doing so experience the thrill of power. These students who perceive themselves to be victims, downtrodden by the school authorities, find 'the rush' of confrontation intoxicating and irresistible. They are adroit at leading the teacher on a wild goose chase and instinctively know how to hijack a class by asking irrelevant questions as outlined above. If the teacher is unwise enough to attempt to respond to these questions, they will 'hop on the bandwagon' with bolder supplementaries which will eventually lead to confusion and disorder. Students as a group love to shout each other down and given the opportunity will shout the teacher down too.

So what are teachers to do when faced with incidents of misbehaviour that challenge their authority? Coercive methods of classroom management as described earlier in this book may have to be used and they can be effective in quelling disorder. Sometimes, they will need to be carried through to the extreme and certain individuals will end up on fixed-term or permanent exclusion. Sometimes, the interest of the class group as a whole demands this. When it is obvious that this appears to be the most likely outcome from the start, failure by teachers or school management to make strong interventions early on does not serve the needs of anyone.

What can be done to help these students?

In the 'qualification race culture' that we have created, parents and school authorities have become locked into a scenario of educational inflation, with little regard being shown for the casualties of such a meritocratic culture. The exam system recognises and rewards only a very narrow range of academic ability. The reality is that a significant minority of students are totally alienated by their experience of school and drop out early.

In some education authorities there is a move to develop an alternative curriculum at KS4 for some pupils outside mainstream education. Individual schools are also considering and implementing ways of integrating elements of an alternative curriculum for students who cannot access the standard curriculum in its current form. Some schools provide a 'golden curriculum' with one or two teachers for much of the day for those Year 7 pupils who require a slower transition from primary to secondary. However, as high truancy rates indicate, there remains a pressing need to differentiate not only the curriculum but also teaching methods themselves, that is to say, the process that goes on within classrooms, in order to make education more accessible and relevant to all. For this, more coherent planning is needed at a policy level to broaden curriculum opportunities in mainstream secondary schools and to gear teaching methods to meet different kinds of learning needs more effectively.

Selection at 11 years remains in some areas and streaming is widespread. This is despite the fact that available research evidence (e.g. Hannon and Boyle 1987, conducted in Ireland) shows clearly that gifted students do at least as well in mixed ability classes as they do in streamed ones, while average and 'weaker' students benefit enormously from the mixed ability situation. The social gain to society of well-run comprehensive schools and mixed ability teaching is significant. From the schools' perspective, mixed ability grouping helps to prevent the development of the delinquent subculture referred to above.

Convincing parents and teachers of the veracity of these findings is difficult. Parents, when it comes to giving their own children whatever competitive advantages possible, worry little about the manifest injustices of our current system. In seeking to gain every competitive advantage possible over others, they invariably vote with their feet and send their children to streamed or selective schools. The ideal of mixed ability teaching is hard to put into effect amongst competing schools, unless there is universal agreement between all the schools in an area or a directive given by the LEA or the Department for Education and Skills.

There are hopeful signs of change in the air. Patronising comments like 'He's great with his hands', or 'She's good at sport/art,' have given way to the recognition of at least eight different intelligences. Howard Gardener and colleagues of 'Project Zero' at Harvard University have studied multiple expressions of human intelligence (Spatial, Bodily-Kinesthetic, Interpersonal, Intrapersonal, Musical), as well as those of the Linguistic-Logical and Mathematical favoured by the current education system. This work has broadened our definition of what intelligence is and recognises the true holistic value of underachieving students.

Some progress has been made in the area of preferred learning styles, although there is still a long way to go. An increasing number of schools assess pupils' learning styles, making students aware of how they can best learn. However, more teachers need an awareness of their own preferred learning style and their consequent natural bias in teaching so they can diversify their approach in order to 'reach', 'speak to' or 'illuminate' learners with styles which differ from their own.

An increased awareness on the part of teachers of the dilemma faced by students who, for whatever reason (physical, social or emotional), cannot cope with the academic demands of school can do much to help. Positive discrimination in terms of school support, e.g. judicious subject provision, and the deployment of teaching personnel with special training, on reduced timetables or increased allowances, for working in these areas, would do much to level the 'educational playing field'.

Many people are beginning to recognise the fact that disruptive children are, in part, a 'by-product' of the education system that we (as a society) operate. In a different context, these students can be just as 'good' as their more academically accomplished peers. This realisation has implications for how we (as teachers) interact with 'problem students'. For the classroom teacher, a 'child-centred approach' in this context may very often mean establishing the kind of relationship with students that is more important than the completion of the task in hand. When teachers relate with students in a way that promotes self-esteem and fosters their own innate motivation, hopes and dreams, it will mean more in the long run than any subject material that can be tested in an examination. Because this is an intangible and nebulous element of teaching, it is often dismissed as being 'aspirational'. This is a pity, because students won't always remember what we taught them but they will never forget how we treated them.

■ Some suggestions on taking mixed ability classes

Teachers experience particular difficulties when teaching classes where there is a wide range of ability among the students. There are arguments for and against mixed ability grouping. As we have said earlier, socially it is better for the students but from the teacher's point of view it is much more difficult to teach a class where the students' ability can range widely. Teachers are familiar with the situation where the bright students have nearly finished an assignment, before the weaker students even get started. Finding enough suitable material for all involves a great deal of preparation because the teacher often has to prepare three lessons for the one class period. It seems that there never is enough time to devote to either the 'high flying' students or those working at the lower level and whenever the teacher sits down with one group the others start clamouring for attention.

It is important that the distinction be made between teaching mixed ability groups and 'mixed ability teaching', which implies a certain teaching method espoused by Kelly (1974) and Davies (1975). Our suggestions here are directed at teachers teaching any subject to a class in which there is a wide range of ability. For the purposes of discussion, students in a mixed ability class can be divided into three types:

1. One group consists of a small number of very able, highly motivated and cooperative students. They are aiming for top grades. They are able to work on their own when required.

2. A second group comprises the main body of students in the class who have average ability and reasonable motivation. They can be taught as a class group. As their motivation and ability to concentrate are limited, they can be left to work on their own for short periods only.

3. A third group might include that small number of students with learning difficulties, who need individual attention. They need constant help, reassurance and guidance. They are unable to work on their own for any length of time without supervision.

In all classes there is a range of ability and varying degrees of motivation among the students, so, in a sense, these categories can apply to any class. However, when teachers speak of the difficulties attendant on teaching mixed ability classes, they are usually referring to classes in which extreme differences occur. Any attempt to teach such a class of students, without taking cognisance of the wide diversity of ability, is just asking for trouble and can be very dispiriting for teachers, who feel that they are getting nowhere.

Before a teacher can begin a programme of work with such a mixed ability class, it may be helpful to consider some of the following.

(a) *A public clarification of goals*

The teacher might, for example, spend some time with the class attempting to clarify what each student wants from school and their level of commitment to studying that subject. It is helpful if everyone is clear from the start that all students are not aiming for the same goal. Some students may be working hard to get good grades at GCSE, then AS and A level, in order to get into university, to pursue specific objectives. Others find the whole studying thing really difficult. They are quite happy to scrape a few GCSEs, because they intend to leave school and enter work, get an apprenticeship, or do day-release at a local college. Yet another group expect to work in a family business. Others have no interest in school or study and intend to leave school as soon as possible. Some cannot cope with school at all.

Each student, in consultation with the teacher, and taking into account his personal ambitions, preferences, talents or family/parental expectations can be encouraged to actively make decisions like choosing the level he wishes to work at. Having done this, it might then be possible to have an open and honest discussion with the class, where each student might reveal to his classmates what he wants from school. The class can be involved in a discussion on how everyone can be helped to get what he wants. This process of making visible the diversity of goals facilitates a more responsible attitude in class. Even if it is only partially successful, it allows the teacher and students to work in an atmosphere with less negative energy than otherwise might be the case.

(b) *A public acceptance of difference*

It is obvious that, while some children are afraid of heights, some are not; that some students are good at sport while others hate it; that some girls find it easy to have boyfriends and others do not. It must be just as obvious that some students are studious and that others lack motivation. People do things in different ways and that has to be accepted.

In this open class discussion, it is important that the weak students accept the 'swots', and that the gifted students accept those who experience difficulties in learning and studying. In an anti-education youth culture where it is not 'cool' to be seen to work hard and achieve, where boys are called 'girls' or 'boffins' if they do and girls are equally ridiculed, it is particularly important to validate effort in any area of school life, including the academic. Tolerance of diversity and appreciation of commonality are valuable things to learn at school. Having established in an open and respectful way that different students have different ambitions, then it follows that there will be different expectations of the different groups and that individual students will approach their studies in different ways. It is perhaps worth mentioning that some students may change their minds during the year. Some, for example, might suddenly discover something they really want to do; others might feel more confident and realise they could achieve more with greater effort and would like to try.

Students are adept at carefully measuring their input. While it may be perfectly reasonable that some students choose to do little or no work, it is important that the choice is made in an honest and open manner. This will ensure that all the students in the class are aware of the context of that student's decision and the long-term consequences of his or her choice.

(c) *In task differentiation*

It is acknowledged that the task cannot be universal. Those students aiming for high grades will be working at a fast pace. They will be working on their own or in small groups. They will be presented with more demanding study material and more will be expected of them in terms of commitment, perseverance, and time spent on homework and coursework. Likewise, other students will need individual attention. They may be given alternative exercises on work cards, or graded parallel exercises, appropriate to their ability. At times they may be doing something quite unrelated to the specific subject being taught.

In preparing lessons for a mixed ability class, the teacher must take these differences into account. Realistic goals must be set so that each group is challenged. For example, in an essay assignment, while a page might be expected from some students, two pages might be expected from the middle group and as much as one can write on the topic from the 'high flyers'. In this way praise and affirmation are accessible to all and not just to the more gifted students. Each group can make progress at its own pace and teachers can stop driving themselves to the edge of distraction trying to make uniform what is diverse.

Because of the open declaration of difference, it is necessary from time to time that the class should engage in cohesion exercises to bond them as a unit. The teacher might organise activities that foster the talents of the academically weak students, their leadership abilities, or their social and organisational skills. These can include activities such as project work with mixed groups, having a table quiz with mixed teams and well chosen questions, using cooperative study methods, going on educational day trips, or undertaking youth enterprise projects. All students need to be valued equally for what they have to offer.

Teaching a class of students with a wide range of ability is hard work. It requires numerous decisions to be made during the course of any lesson when groups and individuals may be engaged in several different activities. Teaching a mixed ability class requires a thorough understanding of individual differences. Teachers need to anticipate difficulties by identifying, for example, those who require more time, those who lack self-confidence and those who are easily bored and impulsive. Interacting with individual students is necessary to secure a high degree of industry from each student, especially those working on their own. This often involves designing appropriate individual assignments and monitoring individual progress. To successfully teach under such conditions demands flexibility and adaptability on the part of the teacher and may be impossible in some subjects when classes are too large.

■ Specific learning difficulties: dyslexia and dyspraxia

Dyslexia and, to a lesser extent dyspraxia, are the specific learning difficulties most commonly associated with learning to read and write. Dyslexia and dyspraxia may co-occur.

Dyslexia is a term used to describe a group of conditions pertaining to a child's inability to process language properly, be it written, spoken or symbolic. It is one of the most frustrating and in many cases debilitating conditions (both emotionally and socially) that can plague the educational development of a child. It is a multifaceted condition which often escapes detection because of its diverse symptoms. It does not manifest itself solely in the academic sphere but involves every aspect of the individual's life. We refer to dyslexia here to draw teachers' attention to the condition and to raise awareness of its manifestation in the behaviour of students who suffer from this condition.

Frequently, dyslexia is not recognised as a specific condition. Children with the condition are labelled stupid, inattentive, lazy, or simply poorly motivated. Parents are confused, teachers are frustrated, and the child is tormented by a sense of failure, isolation, and the knowledge that she is different. Being withdrawn from class, in front of classmates by the special needs teacher or teaching assistant often compounds these feelings of inadequacy, even though it may be the only way that help can be given to the student.

Dyspraxia is sometimes called 'clumsy child syndrome' and it affects a range of fine and gross motor skills. This impacts on handwriting which is poorly formed and, at times, illegible. Students find writing arduous since their arms or hands ache. A pupil may also have difficulties with speech production because of specific difficulties in planning and executing a sequence of voluntary movements.

Dyslexia and dyspraxia involve not only difficulty with reading, writing and mathematics but also include:

- difficulty in understanding words in normal conversation;

- inability to relate to people in groups, or to follow the drift of a conversation;

- a poor sense of direction;

- little or no concept of time;

- inability to concentrate even when involved in a particular activity, such as a game;

- dysequilibrium (balance dysfunction);

- poor motor co-ordination;

- constantly bumping into things or dropping things;

- stuttering, hesitant speech, poor word recall;

- inability to remember names.

A teacher might notice student behaviours such as:

- sharp emotional mood swings;

- need to reread the same word or phrase to get any meaning out of it;

- 'scrawly writing';

- difficulty in following sequential instructions or events;

- difficulty in following motion or moving things (balls, people, traffic);

- various phobias including height, motion-related (e.g. escalators, elevators);

- gets lost easily or all the time;

- unable or unsure in making decisions; doesn't trust one's own ability to do so;

- feelings of inferiority, stupidity, clumsiness;

- inability to organise daily activities, particularly in allocating proper time;

- doing the opposite of what one was told;

- gets drowsy from mental effort, frequently sleepy in class.

What can a class teacher do?

Once teachers are informed or recognise that they have a dyslexic student in the class they can give that child individual attention and reassurance whenever possible. Sensitivity is important. One simple thing teachers can do is to avoid asking the child to read aloud in class. In some circumstances it may be possible to sit with the student and to quietly do a little paired reading. By gently slipping the student the word whenever he hesitates, the teacher can help him achieve some flow in his reading. The focus can then be moved to discussing meanings, exploring ideas or the sharing of reactions and experiences.

These students need the support of teachers in their difficulty. The patience and confidence of the teacher provide a model for them in terms of the patience and confidence they need in themselves. By actively fostering a good relationship with the class as a whole, a teacher can create a climate that will help build a dyslexic student's confidence and self-esteem. This in turn may enable the student to acknowledge his own difficulties (when he is ready to do so) and not be crippled emotionally by the condition.

Teachers can often help a dyslexic student to demystify the text of a subject. Frequently, for example, a math's teacher will find that when the wording of a math's problem has been explained to the student, he is then able to go ahead and do the problem. Very often the students are quite proficient at mathematics once the reading element has been dealt with.

Until recently there hasn't been a lot that can be done for these children other than making sure that they have individual remedial help and personal tutors to help them along. The Department for Education and Skills makes allowances for the more severe cases in the state examinations, but the mild cases continue to suffer, truant, or just opt out within the school system, quietly underachieving and leaving school as soon as possible. Others turn to disruptive behaviour and are perceived as a 'behaviour problem', their learning needs never having been adequately assessed, understood or met.

A new treatment, Applied Kinesiology, claims that it can help the condition by dealing with the integration of the nervous system and body functions. Many successful people in society suffer from dyslexia. Most report difficult times at schools, where inconsiderate and ignorant teachers seemed to take every opportunity to call attention to their 'appalling spelling'. Nonetheless, their innate intelligence shone through where it really matters – in the real world.

Details of organisations that provide information about dyslexia and dyspraxia, and centres offering specialist SpLD training courses, are given in Appendix 3. For additional discussion and information concerning SpLD see MacGrath (1998).

Part 4

Teaching as a Career

Ours is a hope profession. Children are the messages we give to a time we cannot see.

Anon

◼ **Phases in the teaching career**

Teachers go through different phases in their careers. At each stage they bring particular strengths to their role as teacher. The kind of relationships they enter into with students are similarly influenced by age and experience. Each stage of development brings with it its own challenges and frustrations. In outlining the different phases, it hardly needs to be stated that there are no pure stages. However, in our experience we have found that when teachers look back on their careers they remember going through some of the following phases.

Training stage

The enthusiasm and energy of the trainee teacher mark this stage. They will have spent 14 years watching their teachers at school and will have formed some ideas of their own as they face the challenge of crossing the divide between being a student and a teacher.

Some have difficulty in assuming their new role as the one who is in charge of others, in issuing instructions to students or in taking responsibility for the conduct of a class. Others take to the new role with a relish. They love the idea of having some power and control. They set out as one on a mission, fired by a vision, confident that they will, not just make a difference, but change the world. To help them make that transition and to develop the necessary skill in instruction they undergo a course of training.

The ways into teaching vary considerably, as do the quality of the training and the kinds of experience gained. For undergraduates, there is the four-year BEd. For graduates, there is the PGCE and the Graduate Teacher Programme. The one-year full-time or two-year part-time PGCE is by nature very different from the 24-week Graduate Teacher Programme in which you are based in a school receiving school-centred initial teacher training from lead teachers whilst learning 'on the job'. As well as the courses themselves varying, so will any teaching practice you do in schools. The support and consideration you receive at this time can differ greatly depending on the ethos of the school and the personalities within and organisation of the department you join. Some departments are very welcoming and supportive. Others can leave you very much to your own devices, responding if you ask for help but offering little spontaneously.

In considering which route to choose, it is worth thinking about which approach will most help you not only to deliver a curriculum, since it is possible to do this whilst leaving the students behind, but what will actually best equip you to help young people learn. Does the training cover the subject of preferred learning styles, including ideas on how to teach to involve all types? Does it deal adequately with specific learning and other difficulties, not just theoretically but in practical ways that prepare you for meeting students with these difficulties in your classes? Does it consider how to work in real partnership with parents? Does it give guidance and supervised practice in managing classes, preventing and dealing with troublesome behaviour and building constructive relationships with young people? Does it provide ample opportunity to observe skilled teachers and to try out teaching with guidance and support? In a sense, learning how to teach has elements in common with learning how to ride a horse or drive a car. The learner needs to be able to 'try it for themselves' under the tutelage of an experienced practitioner. Generally speaking, the more of this kind of support you get the better.

'Apprentice'

This is the stage that describes the young teacher's first few years of service. The first appointment to a permanent position in a school and having one's own timetable, classes and programme of work is an exciting time for new teachers. They face challenges and difficulties in areas such as classroom discipline, motivating students, dealing with individual differences, assessing students' work, dealing with parents, organising classwork and problems with individual students. For the first year, of course, the Newly Qualified Teacher will have the added stress of still being in their induction year. Support from the induction programme and, very importantly, peer support from others in a similar situation can help erode any sense of isolation and the fear that no one else finds starting to teach a challenge.

Apprentice teachers, though they lack experience, have great enthusiasm and energy at their disposal to enable them to try and get on top of the job, to prove to themselves that they can do it and to achieve a measure of acceptance from their colleagues, the students and the head. A teacher at this stage, frequently without the responsibility of a family and other commitments, is often very active in the life of the school and involved in many extracurricular activities after school hours. Such young teachers, starting out full of enthusiasm and energy, can often have a tremendously positive influence on students and on staff dynamics in general.

Consolidation stage

After teaching for a few years and having taken a number of classes through to their examinations, the next stage in a teacher's career development begins to unfold. The focus now moves to improving skills and competencies, as the teacher attends inservice courses and tries out new materials, methods and teaching strategies. Teachers, at this stage, are more likely to be successful when they attempt the more advanced teaching techniques they came across when training. The success they experience is an important element in building their own confidence as professionals.

During this time, the person makes a commitment to stay in the profession, applying for threshold status as soon as they can. They may settle down at a particular school and begin to consolidate their position, finding an equilibrium between their school and personal life.

Professional stage

This stage is associated with those who, having mastered the skills of classroom teaching, see themselves as confident and competent teachers. They have developed a personal style of teaching and of relating with students.

In order to fulfil their need for power, involvement, and status within the school, they apply for any posts or promotions that may arise or for Advanced Skills Teacher status. Some get recognition at this point. Those who do not, though they might feel hurt, try to keep their morale up and get on with their work. However, the seeds of later personal disillusionment and staff divisions can often begin at this stage. In these circumstances, deserving teachers who fail to be promoted or get recognition, tend to disengage from the school. Though continuing to do their work faithfully, they apply their energies elsewhere, as in union activities, sporting or political organisations, ancillary careers, or hobbies. Others move school or simply leave the profession in frustration.

Mid-career stage

The late 30's and 40's herald the mid-career crisis. By now, the physical and emotional demands of the job begin to show. The cumulative effects of any career disappointments and life's hurts are more difficult to conceal. Teachers can experience periods of frustration with the day-to-day demands of the job and disillusionment with the teaching profession in general. They find themselves asking, 'Is this it? Is there nothing else to aim for but the pension and retirement?' Job satisfaction tends to sink to a career low. There is a real danger that the teacher will get stuck in a rut and settle for what is bearable. There is a choice to be made between stagnating and discovering new horizons.

For better or worse, some choose stagnation. Many reorient them-selves, and try to find new meaning in their work and life. The undertaking of a post-graduate course of study at college or the Open University can be a useful catalyst in this process. This is a critical time. A teacher's success or failure in discovering new dimensions can have a significant influence on his teaching. A fearful, rule-bound, institutionalised teacher (or head), working in a mindless, mechanical way, will fail to inspire students (or staff). When teachers get 'stuck', they stagnate. The system does not pro-vide for this eventuality. It is unfortunate that no mechanism has been found whereby teachers who are 'stuck' can be supported and helped to develop and move on. Thankfully, teachers can do things to help them-selves in this situation and we explore these possibilities in the next section. At this point, we merely wish to draw attention to the mid-career phase in a general way, so that it can be approached with awareness.

Reflective practitioner

Once a teacher succeeds in 'crossing the desert' of the mid-career stage, a period of serenity and relaxed self-acceptance can develop. Any loss in energy and enthusiasm is compensated for by a greater sense of confi-dence and assurance. A shift begins to develop in one's perspective, from a 'time-since birth' with unlimited potential ahead, to an accept-ance of the limitations and finiteness of self and life. Priorities change and things tend to balance themselves out. Teachers in their 50's have lived long enough, and amassed sufficient experience to develop per-spective and take a long-term view of issues that arise in the school.

Retirement stage

This stage used to be thought of as beginning on a teacher's sixtieth or sixty-fifth birthday. However, with the increased physical demands of teaching in the last ten years, more and more teachers are opting for early retirement in their 50's. This can be a period of pleasant reflection or bitter resentment, depending on the teacher's own experience in their particular school, and over the previous 30 to 40 years' teaching generally. Most teachers recommend that one should retire before one is 'broken'. There is a life after school!

■ Minding ourselves

If the teachers don't get fed, they'll eat the children.

Teaching is a stressful occupation. A teacher in the classroom is 'on stage' when they stand before a class. The student audience is highly critical, often apathetic, and mostly there perforce. With 'good' classes, it is possible to have some audience participation. With difficult classes, there is continuous competition for the limelight. There are times when having worked hard for half an hour to get the students' attention you feel that things are finally going your way. Progress is being made. Then suddenly, the school bell rings. Time is up. Lesson is over. Your audience is gone! The next group is 'cold' and you have to begin the same process from the start again. No actor would be able to maintain this kind of performance for very long. It is difficult to sustain the effort for five, six or seven classes in a row. However, there is no place to hide because, when left to themselves, many student groups go completely wild.

Teaching burns an enormous amount of energy. The apparent short working day and long holidays are not the luxury that outsiders sometimes imagine. Without them no one would survive the stress of teaching for long. When teachers are young they have plenty of energy available to do the job and get through the day. However, as they get older, every teacher is susceptible to 'burn out'. Some are forced, because of physical or mental exhaustion, to take time out, while others struggle on for years. The system shows no mercy to these. Students cruelly and relentlessly torment them. Often, at staff level, they are blamed by colleagues for not being able to control their classes, and they become more and more alienated from the decision-making processes of the school.

All teachers experience burn out to some degree during the course of their teaching lives. It is best understood as a kind of progressive, cumulative exhaustion. The symptoms are things which we all experience in normal life, so we are familiar with them. What characterises burn out is their persistent nature and their intensity.

At first it is hardly noticeable, just little things. People often remember that for them it began with their experiencing difficulty in sleeping at night and of feeling confused and forgetful. They found it difficult to relax and stop their minds racing. Many noted that they felt irritable and easily provoked, pessimistic and generally negative about everything. Failure to keep things in perspective was also noted.

For other teachers, the symptoms were more obviously physical in nature. These included persistent headaches, back pain, stomach or bowel problems, that tended to disappear or clear up during holiday times.

In attempting to keep a balance, teachers resort to the same things as everyone else. Not surprisingly, addiction issues arise, particularly in relation to smoking, alcohol, or the habitual use of tranquillisers.

When the day-to-day running of your life is becoming a daunting, exhausting and unfulfilling struggle, any trauma can become the 'straw that broke the camel's back'. Burn out is often precipitated by a family bereavement, caring for aging parents, sick relatives, or young children, or the added stress of an Ofsted visit. Such difficulties can be compounded by problems in relationships and financial worries. These stresses, when combined with the daily demands of teaching, can take their toll even on the most robust individuals.

In many work situations, when someone feels under stress they can put their head down, go silent, and concentrate on doing their job. If they work in an office, no one is likely to be deliberately unplugging their 'phone, trying to rob their keys, deliberately hiding their files, laughing at and making fun of them to their faces, or threatening to damage property around them. When dealing with difficult, demotivated students, the 'unwell' teacher is often routinely faced with this kind of harassment. Not surprisingly, absenteeism can be a problem in schools, and is accounted for in terms of 'sickness' or other ABT (I'll do Anything But Teach) behaviours.

The Teacher Support Line (see Appendix 1) has been set up to help teachers who find themselves in difficult circumstances.

■ Strategies for thriving in the job

Some teachers continue not just to survive, but to enjoy their work right up to their retirement. When asked to account for their continued enthusiasm and good physical health, we have found that they usually make reference to some of the following.

Physical exercise

To thrive in this demanding profession teachers need to build into their daily and weekly routines activities that reduce the cumulative effects of stress. On a physical level it doesn't matter what it is as long as you're doing something that is physically (as opposed to mentally) demanding and that helps you to keep fit. Teachers commonly mention golf, aerobics, tai chi, horse riding, karate, swimming, walking, cycling, dancing, yoga, mountain walking, tennis, sailing and jogging.

Planned relaxation

Many teachers feel that it is also beneficial (if not essential) to have a planned daily routine of deep relaxation. Again, it does not matter what method one uses as long as it works for you. Teachers have talked about things like meditation, prayer, yoga, shiatsu and reiki massage. The main idea is that you need to have a quiet place to go to and be in a position to unwind completely – to go silent within.

Older teachers find it helpful to take a nap when they get home after school. This allows them to unwind and to revitalise themselves.

Personal development

Much of the stress that arises in teaching is influenced by our own emotional state. Teachers often become too caught up in student misbehaviour and allow themselves to get drawn into situations that they would do better to avoid. It can be difficult to be objective when swept up in the emotional whirlwind these situations generate.

There are many personal development courses available that help teachers to increase their own self awareness so that they can remain professionally detached and effective when confronted by the more traumatic elements of school life. Many teachers have found that these courses have helped them to improve their classroom management practices, thus enabling them to teach with less strain and effort. (See Appendix 1.)

Getting support

Teachers are generally willing to help each other but are unlikely to intervene, unless invited to do so. If a teacher finds the going difficult or is in trouble with a particular class, it is important that they seek help immediately. There is nothing to be gained from continuing, week after week, pretending that everything is fine, although it is not easy to admit a problem in a school where others 'seem' to manage. It is even harder to do so in an educational culture of blame, criticism and Ofsted, rather than one of training, skill sharing and support.

It is, however, important that teachers monitor one another. This can amount to a kind of 'peer supervision' which is an accepted practice in some caring professions. It is a great help if a teacher has a few colleagues with whom he can discuss problems, seek advice, or just let off steam and have a laugh. If these colleagues can offer honest feedback, if they have the courage to confront us when necessary, then we are very fortunate indeed. The NUT offers courses on peer coaching. (See Appendix 1.)

Presence

If teachers are not 'grounded' or 'composed' themselves, they can fuel hyperactivity in their students. Having 'wound up' the children, teachers sometimes blame them when they go out of control and prove difficult to manage. More can be achieved if a teacher functions at a sustainable pace. Similarly, by being 'over-strict', a teacher can burn up the available energy in a class on a given day, with the result that the students will 'act up completely' in the next lesson. It is good practice to conserve your energy, to keep your voice soft, to sit down from time to time, and to vary the pace of the lesson.

Older teachers generally appreciate that there are 'tides in the affairs' of school life. There are rhythms to the day, the week, the term, the year and even in the career. Sensitive timing and the ability to 'go with the flow' are part of the performance art that is teaching.

It is also important to be able to listen to the rhythms within oneself. There will be odd days, when for valid reasons, you are not up to the mark. Rather than pressing on regardless, it is prudent on these occasions to fall back on a preprepared emergency strategy. It is a good idea to have a stock of educational videos or puzzles ready that can be used to tide one over.

A quiet refuge

Teachers work under scrutiny. The students are constantly watching and engaging them in dialogue. It is important that teachers are able to take a quiet moment during the day to let go of the feeling of being observed and of needing to be in control. Some schools have rooms available for that specific purpose but in most schools it is difficult to find a suitable place.

It is also worthwhile to be aware that, despite being in the company of lots of people, teaching is essentially a lonely profession. Over the years a teacher spends hours and hours in the company of the same age group of young people, in a role where the relationship has to be one-sided. Contact with adult company is restricted to rushed coffee breaks and lunchtimes.

Beware of perfectionism

Teachers, by and large, strive to do the 'right thing'. They spend a lot of time looking for perfection and correcting mistakes. One of the occupational hazards of teaching is that sometimes they get stuck in a 'correcting, improving, self-righteous' mode of being, which is too narrow to allow for human frailties. Our focus here is mainly on the effect that this syndrome has on the teacher, ignoring for the moment the unfortunate victims of their concern. Some teachers work themselves to the bone, even to the extent that they break themselves physically or mentally. They evaluate their own worth solely in terms of their students' performance in state examinations. Their need to prove themselves takes precedence over everything else. If this level of manic commitment is either ignored, or held in high regard by the school head, parents, and students, these teachers eventually get hurt. Should they fall ill and need to take sick leave, they are likely to be horrified by how easily they have been replaced and by how little the system cares for them. Life just rolls on without them! Our worth as human beings and as teachers is not measured solely by the exam successes of our students. From time to time we all need to step back and try to evaluate our level of commitment, our operating style and, of course, our motivation in doing what we do.

As a profession we need to beware of the danger of rashly evaluating and judging others. The fact that young single teachers, with no family responsibilities, can stay in school every evening correcting, can organise the school concert or travel away with the football team, may mean simply that they have lots of free time. Their wholehearted commitment to the school should not be seen to reflect on the input of older teachers who may be constrained by family or other responsibilities from participating more fully in extracurricular activities. These older teachers nonetheless, by virtue of their presence and experience, make an equally valid contribution to the life of the school.

Being sensitive to the humanity of other people is vital in any team effort. When we are fit and healthy it is important that we are available to help colleagues when they need our support. It is well for us to bear in mind that in a few years' time, however competent we are now, we may be depending on others to help us through a tough year, while we recover from an illness, bereavement or some other trauma.

Honouring our professional integrity

Earlier in this book we described teaching as craft; a process through which skills are employed in order to arrive at preconceived ends. Later we tried to show that in many respects teaching is a creative art in which the end achieved is emergent, discovered through action. Many of the decisions and judgements teachers make are based largely on intuitions and adaptations that arise in the course of action. Teachers, in order to cope with unforeseen contingencies, are often required to function in an innovative way, guided by their own educational values and personal beliefs.

Some teachers experience a sense of 'dis ease' – an internal struggle – as they try to reconcile certain contradictions inherent in the job. These contradictions arise often because of an ideological clash between different views of education. One vision of education is that it is a process devoted to the personal development of the individual, in a free and democratic setting. Another view sees education as a response to the requirements of the market-place, whereby students must learn a certain body of knowledge in order to gain employment. This ideological conflict within education treats as problematic the curriculum, pedagogic practice, assessment procedures and management styles, both in the classroom and in the administration of the schools. This underlying discord exists not only at the level of ideology but also in the day-to-day realities and praxis of school life. Many schools are essentially custodial and authoritarian, based on a hierarchical view of power, knowledge and language. A teacher working in these schools must contend with the residual conservatism of the profession, the selective and reproductive function of the education system and the impossibility of escaping the forms of social relationship required by society.

Within the past decade more and more teachers have been preoccupied with questions of classroom control and management, and with the preservation of their own personal and professional well-being. Most teachers adapt to their particular situation by meeting the system on its own terms. Achieving 'good results' and, on the strength of the reputation thus acquired, they introduce some variations in curriculum and pedagogy.

Teachers are well aware of the limitations of what they are doing and of the limits within which they work. They need to get something more out of teaching than a pay packet and the knowledge that their students do well. What many desire is the space to be creative. If they are denied this, they often become cynical and bitter, deriving little satisfaction from what they do and seeking fulfillment elsewhere. Unless schools provide for teachers' continued growth through collaborative and collegial systems of management, the existence of optimal conditions for the educational development of students cannot be assured.

References

Davies, R. P. (1975) *Mixed Ability Grouping*. London: Temple Smith.

Edwards, A. V. and Furlong, V. J. (1978) *The Language of Teaching*. London: Heinemann.

Gardner, H. (1991) *The Unschooled Mind: How children Think and How Schools Should Teach*. New York: Basic Books.

Glasser, W. (1969) *Schools Without Failure*. New York: Harper & Row.

Glasser, W. (1985) *Control Theory in the Classroom*. New York: Harper & Row.

Hannan, D. and Boyle M. (1987) *Schooling Decisions: The Origins and Consequences of Selection and Streaming in Irish Post-Primary Schools*. Dublin: Dublin Economic and Social Research Institute.

Hargreaves, D. Hestor, S., Mellor, F. (1975) *Deviance in Classrooms*. London: Routledge and Kegan Paul.

Humphries, T. (1995) *A Different Kind of Teacher*. Cork: published privately.

Kelly, A. V. (1974) *Teaching Mixed Ability Classes*. London: Harper & Row.

Kounin, J. (1977) *Discipline and Group Management in Classrooms*. New York: Holt, Rinehart & Winston.

MacGrath, M. (1998) *The Art of Teaching Peacefully*. London: David Fulton Publishers.

Marland, M. (2002) *The Craft of the Classroom*. London: Heinemann.

Ó Suilleabháin, S. (1986) 'Towards our professional identity', in P. Hogan (ed.) *Willingly to School?: Perspectives on Teaching as a Profession in Ireland in the Eighties*. Dublin: Educational Studies Association of Ireland.

Williams, K. (1989) The case for democratic management in schools', *Irish Educational Studies*, **8**(2), 76.

Appendix 1

The Teacher Support Line offers a national, confidential counselling support and advice service.

The Teacher Support Line England: 08000 562 561.

The Teacher Support Line Cymru: 0800 085 5088.

The National Union of Teachers runs a range of professional and some personal development courses and peer coaching for members and non-members. For information contact:

CPD Programme

Education and Equal Opportunities Department

Hamilton House, Mabledon Place, London WC1H 9BD

0207 388 6191

Appendix 2

Primary feelings

Bothered	Disappointed	Afraid	Exhausted
Unhappy	Bored	Fearful	Ashamed
Sad	Confused	Terrified	Guilty
Bad	Puzzled	Insecure	Helpless
Troubled	Uneasy	Nervous	Lonely
Miserable	Concerned	Emotional	Left out
Upset	Worried	Vulnerable	Hurt
Depressed	Anxious	Tired	Uncomfortable
Down	Frightened	Stressed out	
Frustrated	Scared	Embarrassed	

Secondary feelings

Angry	Mad	Resentful	Infuriated
Annoyed	Bitter	Outraged	Aggravated
Furious			